鼠牛虎兔龍蛇馬羊猴雞犬豬

CHINESE SEXUAL ASTROLOGY

Eastern Secrets
to
Mind-Blowing Sex

By

SHELLY WU

NEW PAGE BOOKS
A division of The Career Press, Inc.
Franklin Lakes, NJ

Copyright © 2007 by Shelly Wu

CHINESE SEXUAL ASTROLOGY
EDITED BY KIRSTEN DALLEY
TYPESET BY KRISTEN PARKES
Cover design by Lu Rossman/Digi Dog Design NYC
Printed in the U.S.A. by Book-mart Press
Illustrations in Appendix A by Sheridah Davis

To order this title, please call toll-free 1-800-CAREER-1 (NJ and Canada: 201-848-0310) to order using VISA or MasterCard, or for further information on books from Career Press.

The Career Press, Inc., 3 Tice Road, PO Box 687,
Franklin Lakes, NJ 07417
www.careerpress.com
www.newpagebooks.com

Library of Congress Cataloging-in-Publication Data

Wu, Shelly, 1959-
    Chinese sexual astrology : eastern secrets to mind-blowing sex / by Shelly Wu.
       p. cm.
    Includes index.
    ISBN-13: 978-1-56414-921-3
    ISBN-10: 1-56414-921-8
      1. Sex instruction. 2. Astrology, Chinese. I. Title.

HQ31.W965 2007
613.9ʹ6--dc22

                                         2006025974

To the many friends, colleagues, and students who have been so supportive, asked the great questions, and inspired me daily. And as always, a special thank you to Aristotle—my husband, best friend, and lover:

"Here's to old Dogs learning new tricks."

鼠牛虎兔龍蛇馬羊猴雞犬猪

Contents

鼠牛虎兔龍蛇馬羊猴鷄犬猪

INTRODUCTION

*Love is of all passions the strongest, for it attacks
simultaneously the head, the heart and the senses.*

—Lao Tzu (Laozi)

Whether a mind-blowing quickie or an orgasmic marathon, few things can equal the intense pleasure of love and sex. The heart-pounding thrill of romantic love is a universal human pursuit; we have all loved and lost and loved and won, but mostly we have just loved. Indeed, love is the universal language and the very essence of our being. Therefore, there comes a time when most of us are faced with the pivotal decision of choosing a partner. This is a decision that will affect our chance for relationship happiness and future sexual satisfaction.

From the earliest Chinese records, the sex act between a man and a woman was seen as a powerful and essential force that controlled the universe. According to the Tao Te Ching, sexual energy is the force in nature that keeps the "earth circling the heavens." The merging of man and woman—yang and yin—was thought to be of the highest spiritual realms and a reflection of an organized and sacred universe. Therefore, the importance of making love was highly emphasized, not only for physical well-being and longevity, but for emotional and spiritual cultivation as well.

Thousands of years ago, the ancient Chinese understood the need for sex education. They had "pillow books," popular wedding gifts for young couples containing everything from astrological compatibility to erotic suggestions for igniting passion. These erotic and exquisitely detailed books were meant to be tucked under the pillow of a young bride; they completed her trousseau and were meant for her and her lover's education and excitement. These books taught couples to be generous with each other—not merely for enjoyment, but to fulfill the man's essential need for the woman's yin energy and the woman's concurrent need for the man's yang essence.

In contrast to the misogynistic sexual repression of women common in many other ancient (and modern) cultures, Taoist masters encouraged the complete satisfaction of a woman sexually. Young men were taught that to ensure their own satisfaction, and for the balance of yin and yang to occur, they must seek to satisfy their lover completely. This attitude of sexual wholesomeness stood in stark contrast to some of the Western views of sex. In the East, sex was a health issue and not a moral one. Eastern sages and medical doctors extolled the sexual act for health and happiness, while their Western equivalents imbued sex with the oppressive and repressive rhetoric of caveats, restrictions, and taboos.

The Chinese obsession with, and celebration of, the erotic is graphically demonstrated in Chinese art, archaeological records, and ancient literary sources. From the erotic imagery of 200 B.C. tomb decorations to the 10th century crystal penis on display at the Museum of Ancient Chinese Sexual Culture in Tongli, the extraordinary role that sexuality played in the daily lives of the Chinese people is explicitly evident. While the art of love in ancient China appeared to be phallic-oriented, it was widely believed that sexual intercourse enhanced one's internal spiritual practice and unified the physical with the spiritual—something that would be of benefit to both sexes. Moreover, misogyny against women was virtually unheard of in China until much later in the country's history. The Chinese have a long and rich history of celebrating their sexuality in a positive and healthy way. The art of sexuality was practiced with the goal of transforming the mundane into a higher spiritual plane—the ultimate intent being oneness with each other and with the natural world.

Recently in the West, there has been an ever-increasing awareness of the importance of fusing our spiritual, mental, and physical energies in order to achieve complete satisfaction. This awareness has yielded an explosion of renewed interest in ancient erotic manuals, such as the *Secrets of the Jade Bed Chamber* from China, the *Kama Sutra* from India, and the *Ishimpo* from Japan. In a quest to reconnect with passion and enrich their sexual experience, many couples are exploring Taoist, Tantric, and astrological compatibilities regarding sexuality.

Love and Sex Written in the Stars

For many of us, the burning question remains: Why do some singe their wings on love's flames, while others glide through romance unscathed? In order to answer this, we can look to the time-tested wisdom of Chinese astrology and apply it to our relationships and sexuality. Chinese astrology is based on 12 archetypal temperaments, and provides enlightenment for, and insight into, our most intimate relationships. The Chinese astrological system reveals attributes, driving forces, and possibilities. It is an interpretive art built upon the foundations of principle, order, and the spiritual laws of synchronicity, an art that will help us map out the journey of our spirit through the physical dimensions of personality and purpose.

In ancient China, the leaders of the time were responsible for maintaining the spiritual, mental, and physical health of the people. After many centuries of recording philosophical, behavioral, and natural earth phenomena, theories concerning human sexuality also began to form. Many of the ancient sexual practices were secretive and arcane in nature, and only passed along orally from teacher to student. The Eastern Zodiac is the oldest known astrological system in the world. Ancient writings have been dated as early as the 4th millennium B.C., and can be found in the monasteries of Tibet, China, and Southeast Asia. Multitudes have consulted this timeless system, and it remains as pertinent today as it was many centuries ago.

The phrase "lucky in love" is a rather ambiguous expression. Most of us know what love is and are acutely aware if it's "working" or not. Although this "love luck" cannot be seen, it is profoundly evident in our daily lives. In Eastern philosophy, there are three types of luck: "Heavenly love luck" is our romantic fate, that unseen network of compatibility connections and the spiritual love map of our life. "Human love luck" represents the paths and partners we choose using our free will. (It's important to remember that the universe will never thwart our choices even if this means certain disaster.) Finally, "earthly love luck" consists of manipulating romance by the arrangement of our environment and external influences, using tools such as feng shui, talismans, colors, and scents, as well as auditory and visual arousal. Physicists tell us that "for every action, there is an equal and opposite reaction." The laws of earthly physics function in a similar fashion throughout the spiritual world, so one might say that Chinese sexual astrology is a form of "romantic quantum physics." Just as gravity causes an object to plummet to the ground, so the laws of romantic physics dictate that for every act, there is a logical consequence. In this way we make or break our relationships, not just through random "luck," but also through our behavior.

According to ancient Chinese wisdom, there are two facets that make up personality. The first is "temperament"—our predisposition. The second is "character"—the actual disposition we acquire after we are born. Spiritual temperament plus earthly character equals personality. Truly, our character reflects the intent of our heart. Character traits that we would view as positive—fidelity, passion, attachment—reflect the alignment of our body with our spirit (qi). Traits we would view as negative—selfishness, sadism, neglect—reflect a significant separation between our personality and our spiritual essence. We have all known those individuals whose personalities seem completely divorced from their spiritual selves. In love and in life, the greater the gulf between one's spirit and personality, the darker the character.

Each Chinese astrological sign or archetype is a balanced mixture of positive and negative sexual attributes. For example, the Snake's legendary sexual prowess and breathless eroticism can also manifest as philandering or a wandering eye; the Ox's marathon lovemaking and slow hand can also become undemonstrative or passionless; and the Pig's all-encompassing sensuality can also be expressed as fetishism or bawdy behavior.

The Asian Zodiac uses calculations of yearly or lunar-year periods, rather than months, to order and arrange the signs. Each of the 12 animal signs lasts for an entire year, beginning on various dates between mid-January through mid-February. Some of the sub-specialties of Chinese astrology—such as the Four Pillars of Destiny (Ba Zi)—use the first day of spring (Li Chun, which falls on February 4 or 5 each year) as a beginning date for certain calculations. Each sign repeats every 12th year, but the specific combination of animal sign and element occurs only once every 60 years.

Our Chinese astrological signature offers an intimate look into our most private sexual world. Each of the 12 Chinese astrological signs has its own unique sexual style, preferred pleasurable sensations, and turn-ons. (If you do not know what your Chinese birth sign is, please consult Appendix B). In Part I of this book, we will explore the unseen chemistry that long-lasting relationships are made of. In Part II, we will examine the role that our mind, intellect, and attitude play in preparing to make memorable love. And in Part III, we will delve into the secret sexual world of each of the 12 animal archetypes, and peek into the deliciously naughty, the tame, the tawdry, and sometimes even the taboo physical side of our karmic love connections. (I had initially considered omitting some practices which could be considered controversial or might seem shocking to some. After consideration, I decided to stay as close as possible to traditional Taoist sexual cultivation and let you, the reader, decide what is valuable.)

While any relationship can work, passion, romance, and attachment flow more smoothly when we are in tune with the natural laws of the universe. Chinese sexual astrology contains tried-and-true advice that combines spiritual compatibility with physical pleasures. From your first conversation with your partner to orgasmic euphoria, I hope this book will become your friend and erotic adviser on your path to love. Welcome to a new world of thinking and possibilities—love and sex written in the stars!

Wishing you a satisfied spirit, mind, and body,

SHELLY WU

Author's Note

The two most popular romanization styles of Chinese characters and words are pinyin and Wade-Giles. Pinyin has largely supplanted the older Wade-Giles system, and thus has become the standard system for romanizing the Chinese language. For sake of clarity and ease of pronunciation, pinyin will be used throughout this text. (In instances in which readers would more familiar with the Wade-Giles spelling, this version will be given as well.)

Some comparative conversions from Wade-Giles to pinyin:

Wade-Giles	Pinyin
ch'i	qi
tao	dao
chi	ji
t'ai	tai
t'ien	tian
t'ao	tao

PART 1

SPIRIT CONNECTIONS

To love deeply gives you strength.
Being loved deeply gives you courage.

—Laozi

CHAPTER 1

鼠牛虎兔龍蛇馬羊猴鷄犬猪

CHINESE LOVE SIGNS— KARMIC CONNECTIONS

I BELIEVE IN ONLY MEANINGFUL COINCIDENCES. The time that our spirits choose to enter this physical world is both significant and informative. When we first encounter someone, our eyes meet and we see their hair color, eyes, and smile, but we also "see," or sense, their spirit energy or qi (chi). Physical appearance, professional aspirations, or social circumstances cannot explain the intense attraction that exists between certain souls. This attraction is not based on sexual chemistry alone (although that element is often present); rather, it is a "spiritual rendezvous" between kindred or familiar spirits.

It has been said that there is a special someone for all of us. Actually, there are many "special someones" with whom we could be very happy. However, there comes a time when most of us yearn to unite with one kindred spirit. While *any* relationship is possible, given enough understanding and maturity, Eastern sages have known for millennia that certain souls seek out each other and become powerfully attached. In Eastern culture, the spirit or soul is of utmost importance, and it is through the ongoing process of love relationships that we become whole. Therefore, it is important to cultivate these spiritual connections in order to harmoniously merge our minds, and subsequently our sexual energies, with another person.

The following relationship guidelines are time-tested and true through thousands of years of experience.

What Is a Karmic Connection?

A karmic connection is a powerful psychic connection and a tangible chemistry between two people. It is the successful reuniting of spirit, mind, and body with a matching/kindred/familiar soul, and an ongoing relationship that our spirit picks up time and again and in various guises and places. While it is sometimes true that opposites attract each other, more often than not, like attracts like. Kindred or familiar souls always gravitate toward each other and seek to reunite once again. These relationships can occur between spouses, between parents and children, between best friends, between work colleagues, and even between ourselves and a beloved pet. However, those that occur within the context of a sexual or love relationship are extraordinarily profound.

Where Will I Find My Soul Mate?

Significant people come into our lives at appointed times. As we are presented with many choices throughout our lives, there are also many individuals who will, in their own way, take us down a certain life path. Each potential partner carries their own unique combination of spirit-improving or spirit-destroying potentials. Is searching for one's soul mate a gamble of sorts? Definitely. But by using the universal principles of Chinese astrology we can make more-informed decisions about who might be a better bet for us to further our spiritual, mental, and physical happiness.

As we are spiritual creatures contained within a mutable, physical body, our ultimate purpose in this earthly existence is spiritual or soul development. Love, enticement, and affection all originate at a soul level. The closest experience we can have with our Creator is through the experience of loving others; indeed, it is through the selfless act of giving with no thought of getting anything in return that we can glimpse the very essence of our Creator and nurture the very best of ourselves. A true soul mate can be identified as one who walks alongside of us in support and agreement of purpose. Soul mates share a life goal and steadfastly work together to achieve it. On the darker side, potential, joy, and one's higher purpose can all be destroyed by uniting with the wrong individual.

A spiritual connection is the first and most crucial support for a successful mental and physical relationship. In order to have a fulfilling physical union and a lasting friendship, this critical first step in the spirit, mind, and body connection cannot be skipped or ignored. All superior and truly fulfilling sexual relationships are built upon this cornerstone. However, it is sometimes difficult to differentiate between infatuation, lust, and love. Therefore, one must ask the critical questions: Will a certain romantic alliance make me a better person? Is this a "balanced" relationship of give and take? Or does this attachment elicit only discouragement, continually bringing out the worst in me? Hopefully, the guidelines in this book will assist you in determining whether the people you encounter are potential long-term relationship material, or merely passing attractions that enable you to work through some unfinished business.

We need not look far to find significant connections in our lives. Most of the relationships that we would consider important today can find their origin in past associations. The reality is that there is no need to go searching for our soul mates, as twin souls have an ongoing connection that neither time nor mortality can separate. Whether we identify them in the moment or in retrospect, these karmic relationships will inevitably unfold before us—we have only to recognize them.

These kinds of spiritual and soul mate relationships can occur between same-sex persons as well as in male-female relationships, but both have one thing in common: They are unions in which each couple is brought together to achieve a common goal, and each person contributes to the personal growth of the other. This doesn't mean that two soul mates won't experience friction, however. At times, each may feel that the other person is the source of, rather than the remedy for, their pain. This feeling is due to the fact that the soul mate "mirrors" the other and thus spiritually empowers their partner to develop their strengths and confront their weaknesses. In essence, the soul mate enables their partner to emerge as the whole and fulfilled human being they were meant to be.

Fresh insights, new sets of choices, and new arenas in which to make these choices are the gifts given to us as we identify and pursue our life's purpose and seek spiritual enlightenment. Destiny will assist us and steer that familiar soul into our path, but our fate will be determined by what we do with these opportunities, as well as by the natural consequences of our choices.

Whether you long for a soul mate who will assist you in spiritual growth, or a twin soul who joins with you to complete an important work or purpose, let's continue on and see if any of these connections are occurring in your life right now!

CHAPTER 2

鼠牛虎兔龍蛇馬羊猴鶏犬猪

YIN/YANG—
STILLNESS AND MOVEMENT

THE ANCIENT CHINESE ATTRIBUTED THE SOURCE OF ALL LIFE to
the balance between heaven and earth, the yin and the yang. The yin represents the negative, passive night force—female, water, and receiving.
The yang represents the positive, aggressive, day force—male, fire, and
giving. These two halves, the yin and the yang, are represented in the
familiar Chinese symbol for the tai ji. The two semi-circles of light and
dark that make up the complete tai ji merge into each other and move in
harmony.

One yin and one yang are called Tao (pronounced
"dow"). Meaning "the way," Tao is the ancient Chinese
term for the ordering principle that makes harmony
possible. In the ancient text of the Tao Te Ching, the
Chinese philosopher Laozi formulated a philosophical system that introduced the concept of health and
prosperity through awareness of the natural cosmic cycles. This awareness
of life, he suggested, was the path to finding balance and achieving a
"satisfied mind." According to this principle, the Tao gives birth to one
perfect whole that carries yin on its back and embraces yang in its arms.
This blending of qi then becomes balanced and harmonious. Yin and yang
are the Tao of heaven and earth, and the principle and root beginning of life
and death, of mother and father, and of spiritual enlightenment.

Contained within the light or yang half of the yin/yang symbol is a small circle of dark yin, representing the feminine within the masculine. Similarly, within the dark or yin half of this symbol is a circle of light yang, representing the masculine within the feminine. The yang seeks to find the yin, which in turn is powerfully magnetized toward its other half. Finding out your birth-year polarity (whether you are yin or yang) will reveal which side of the karmic coin you represent. You can discover whether you are, in essence, an ardent front-line yang lover or a dreamy backseat yin lover.

Yang Lovers (+ Movement): Rat, Tiger, Dragon, Horse, Monkey, Dog

Yang lovers take the lead in life and in the bedroom. Their sexual energy builds rapidly and originates in the genitals. This energy needs to be brought out gradually toward the other parts of the body. In love, yang lovers can be quick out of the gate and possess a potent and passionate soul. This positive polarity represents: giving, movement, masculine energy, fire, the sun, daylight, heat, dryness, quickness, assertiveness, angular shapes, the intellect, and the heavens.

Yin Lovers (- Stillness): Ox, Rabbit, Snake, Goat, Rooster, Pig

Yin lovers are receptive, passive lovers who are sensitive, sensual, and feeling-oriented. Their sexual energy originates in the outer areas of the body and needs to be brought in toward the genitals. Yin lovers like to take their time and enjoy the build-up preliminaries in love. This negative polarity represents: receiving, stillness, female energy, the moon, night-time, coolness, moisture, slowness, passivity, receptiveness, round smooth shapes, intuition, and the earth.

Our spirits know no gender, and are much more than the amorphous human expression of masculinity or femininity. According to ancient Chinese wisdom, it is yin or yang essence, and not physical gender, that will influence your sensibilities and inclinations. In this sense, any one of us has the capacity to be either the giver or the receiver. For instance, yin males, such as Rabbits, Goats, or Pigs, possess a yin soul and are able to express their "feminine face" more readily than other men. Yang females, such as Tigers, Horses, and Dogs, possess a yang soul and are able to express their assertive "masculine face" more readily than other women.

After determining whether you are yin or yang, it's time to see where your birth-year animal sign (earthly branch) is placed within the eight major relationship power patterns or energies. In these groupings, notice that some relationships are set up for drama. Those signs with a double whammy of, say, peach blossom and combatant, personify the love/hate relationship. Others, such as the double blessing of being a soul mate and lover in kind, bring harmony and happiness. Familiarize yourself with your sign's unique network of connections and refer back to this section frequently for reference.

Relationship Energies

Rat (+ Yang):

Soul mate to—Ox
In trine with—Monkey, Dragon
In opposition to—Horse
Combatant to—Goat
In kind with—Ox
Resolving karma with—Rabbit
Steed—Tiger
Peach blossom—Rooster

Ox (- Yin):

Soul mate to—Rat
In trine with—Snake, Rooster
In opposition to—Goat
Combatant to—Horse
In kind with—Rat
Resolving karma with—Dragon
Steed—Pig
Peach blossom—Horse

Tiger (+ Yang):

Soul mate to—Pig
In trine with—Horse, Dog
In opposition to—Monkey
Combatant to—Snake
In kind with—Rabbit
Resolving karma with—Snake
Steed—Monkey
Peach blossom—Rabbit

Rabbit (- Yin):

Soul mate to—Dog
In trine with—Goat, Pig
In opposition to—Rooster
Combatant to—Dragon
In kind with—Tiger
Resolving karma with—Horse
Steed—Snake
Peach blossom—Rat

Dragon (+ Yang):

Soul mate to—Rooster
In trine with—Rat, Monkey
In opposition to—Dog
Combatant to—Rabbit
In kind with—Snake
Resolving karma with—Goat
Steed—Tiger
Peach blossom—Rooster

Snake (-Yin):

Soul mate to—Monkey
In trine with—Ox, Rooster
In opposition to—Pig
Combatant to—Tiger
In kind with—Dragon
Resolving karma with—Monkey
Steed—Pig
Peach blossom—Horse

Horse (+ Yang):

Soul mate to—Goat
In trine with—Tiger, Dog
In opposition to—Rat
Combatant to—Ox
In kind with—Goat
Resolving karma with—Rooster
Steed—Monkey
Peach blossom—Rabbit

Goat (-Yin):

Soul mate to—Horse
In trine with—Rabbit, Pig
In opposition to—Ox
Combatant to—Rat
In kind with—Horse
Resolving karma with—Dog
Steed—Snake
Peach blossom—Rat

Monkey (+ Yang):

Soul mate to—Snake
In trine with—Rat, Dragon
In opposition to—Tiger
Combatant to—Pig
In kind with—Rooster
Resolving karma with—Pig
Steed—Tiger
Peach blossom—Rooster

Rooster (-Yin):

Soul mate to—Dragon
In trine with—Ox, Snake
In opposition to—Rabbit
Combatant to—Dog
In kind with—Monkey
Resolving karma with—Rat
Steed—Pig
Peach blossom—Horse

Dog (+ Yang):

Soul mate to—Rabbit
In trine with—Tiger, Horse
In opposition to—Dragon
Combatant to—Rooster
In kind with—Pig
Resolving karma with—Ox
Steed—Monkey
Peach blossom—Rabbit

Pig (- Yin):

Soul mate to—Tiger
In trine with—Horse, Dog
In opposition to—Snake
Combatant to—Monkey
In kind with—Dog
Resolving karma with—Tiger
Steed—Snake
Peach blossom—Rat

CHAPTER 3

鼠牛虎兔龍蛇馬羊猴鶏犬猪

LOVE WRITTEN IN THE STARS— SOUL MATE CONNECTIONS

IF DESIRE, ATTRACTION, AND LOVE ORIGINATE at a soul level, how can we determine if a relationship has long-term potential or is just a passing flame? While some relationships are simply ones of convenience or duty, others are truly karmic in nature. In the relationship energies chart (see Chapter 2), you will find a rapport road map of sorts. Find your sign and see what the karmic connection is.

Soul Mates

The idea of soul mates has existed from time immemorial. Soul mates are the kindred spirits and true spiritual helpmates of the Eastern Zodiac. The soul mate connection is the most potent of the compatibility connections and is comprised of familiar souls attached spiritually from previous associations. They are drawn together in the present because of their association in the past. Within this unforgettable connection we will find our karmic cohorts, our twin souls, and those who will be best suited to assist us in our spiritual development. The attraction between two soul mates is a powerful one, and if separation ensues, neither may fully recover.

These are the most complimentary couples of the Zodiac, and each will be an invaluable asset in, and catalyst to, the other's spiritual growth. Whether you desire a soul mate, who will encourage your spiritual growth,

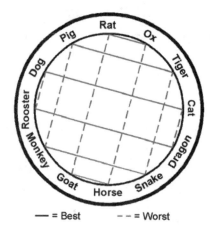

— = Best   - - = Worst

or a "twin flame," who will work side by side with you in a united purpose, it is not necessary to actively search for these relationships, as they tend to unfold before our eyes. When the spirit, mind, and body are ready, the soul mate will appear.

Rat—Ox

Those born into Rat and Ox years are sentimental and vulnerable to each other. These two signs form a mutual admiration society and compliment each other in many ways. Both souls are family- and security-oriented and are drawn together in life and in love. The stable Ox provides consistency and practicality to the Rat's clever ideas and projects. Because they are opposite sides of the same coin, they allow each other to revel in strengths and face weaknesses in a safe emotional environment. While no relationship is perfect, this one promises to be pretty close to ideal for each partner. Growth occurs and problems are overcome, even when the other seems to be the source of the problem.

Tiger—Pig

The deepest of bonds and connections are found between the affectionate Pig and the forthright Tiger. The Pig is never threatened by the Tiger's grand accomplishments and truly enjoys the Tiger's success as if it were their own. In friendship and in love, this relationship is a keeper. These two soul mates can work through nearly any difficulty and walk side by side spiritually, mentally, and physically. Each "reflects" the other, thus allowing deep insight into the inner self. The Tiger's need for change and outside interests combined with the Pig's need for affection and physical comforts makes for a perfect yin/yang communion. Not only can the Tiger and Pig live and love together successfully, but they can also work arm-in-arm as a team in vocational efforts.

Rabbit—Dog

These two souls recognize each other immediately, as most have spiritual links from other times and places. There tends to be an ongoing connection between these two signs that is picked up again and again and in various times and places. A true love connection can be recognized by the "giving" quality of its love, and this kind of selflessness is commonly seen in this karmic connection. Each has the "personal growth curriculum" of the other in the forefront of their heart and mind. If the "attached" Dog and the "detached" Rabbit can overcome their fears and their trust issues, this is a match made in heaven.

Dragon—Rooster

These two soul mates form a life-line for each other. The Dragon's Earth element supports and enables the Rooster's Metal element, thus creating a perfect circuit and a harmonious love match. Both retain their own outside interests independent of the other, yet they form an amicable team and can live in domestic harmony. On the path to love harmony, the Rooster and Dragon may cross paths with each other several times before recognition occurs. The intensity of the connection leaves no doubt that each has indeed found their other half. The Rooster has the spunk and enterprise to hold the interest of the dramatic Dragon, and together they make a handsome and lively couple.

Snake—Monkey

These soul mates seldom tire of their intense physical attraction toward one another. Equally matched in both guile and allure, the Snake and the Monkey must be cautious of infidelities. This is the Richard Burton/ Elizabeth Taylor love connection, one that has been known to be a relationship of many seasons and incarnations. Break-ups and reunions abound, but in the end these two can't live without each other. Their spiritual link will reaffirm itself time and time again. This combination is happiest when they identify what their united purpose is, and work hand-in-hand to accomplish that goal or life mission. These two can be identified by their similar outlooks on life and their respective intimate contributions, with each using their own unique gifts and perspectives. These two have the potential to celebrate a golden wedding anniversary.

Horse—Goat

These two soul mates believe in each other and compliment each other perfectly. The Horse is the personification of the yang, masculine day-force, and the Goat is the very essence of the yin, feminine night-force. The Horse, whether male or female, will embody the yang essence that is the initiating forceful impulse which delineates and defines. The Goat, whether male or female, will embody the yin essence that is the responsive nurturing impulse which responds and reunites. The Horse's decisive mental activity and the Goat's poetic inner life are in true yin/yang communion. Together, these two will share many fulfilling moments when they connect.

CHAPTER 4

鼠牛虎兔龍蛇馬羊猴鷄犬猪

LOVE TRINITIES—
LOVERS IN TRINE

THESE COMPATIBILITY GROUPINGS ARE KNOWN for their affection toward each other and their like-mindedness. They walk hand in hand through the realm of the heart. While soul mates work toward the goal of spiritual development, those signs found in harmonious trine could be described as "twin flames" or "twin souls," who are brought together to achieve a common goal or purpose in this life.

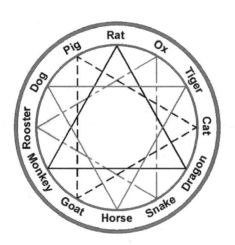

Horse, Tiger, Dog
(Decisiveness, Nobility, Watchfulness)

These high-spirited lovers comprise the compatibility trine of "purpose." These three signs seek one another's company and are like-minded in their pursuit of humanitarian causes. Each excels in verbal communication and is a gifted orator. Relationships and personal connections are their highest priority, and each one seeks their intimate soul mate in this life. Idealistic, decisive, and noble, these three are passionate and earthy lovers ruled by the assertive, positive yang energy.

Tiger—Horse

These two kindred souls are natural friends and lovers. Like-minded in their pursuit of new challenges, the Tiger and Horse speak the same language of action, idealism, and improving the human condition. Each supports the other in their mutual pursuit of making this world a better place. Both are physically active, athletic, and in forward "yang" motion.

Horse—Dog

The Dog and the Horse comprise a remarkable couple. These two effusive souls adore one another and speak the same language of humanity, freedom, and fairness. The vanquishing vigilante meets Robin Hood when these natural-born rebels unite. They may very well find themselves in the limelight or even in the middle of a revolt.

Dog—Tiger

If ever there were a karmic love affair, it would be between these two souls. The Tiger and the Dog are naturally drawn toward one another and interact with encouragement and generosity. The Tiger is the emperor and the Dog, the prime minister. These two have the highest respect for one another and each will run to the aid of the other. Together, they make a determined team that is destined to succeed.

Rat, Dragon, Monkey
(Concealment, Unpredictability, Irrepressibility)

These achievement-oriented and visionary signs comprise the second compatible trinity. They are intense and enthusiastic lovers. In life and in love, these three tend to lean toward restlessness and a single-mindedness of purpose. Impetuous and easily frustrated, these three soul mates are irrepressible, unpredictable, and possess potent, positive yang energy.

Rat—Dragon

When these two are married, emotional security reins supreme. The Dragon and the Rat work well as a team; this is a creative union able to put ideas and plans into practice. The Rat is an organizational genius, while the Dragon is a conjurer of crowds and big projects. They recognize each other's taste for variety and share a love of socializing. This is a close-to-perfect relationship for both.

Dragon—Monkey

These two compatible lovers will "click" immediately as they speak a similar language of excitement and unpredictability. They flow together naturally—the Monkey full of fun and the Dragon full of "presence." As kindred sprits, each brings spontaneity and energy to the union. In love and in life, these two have an excellent chance for a stimulating and enduring relationship.

Monkey—Rat

Sexuality is a gift, a pleasure, and an art between Rats and Monkeys. These two love each other and are not hesitant about showing it. Exhausting nights of love intertwined with intellectual conversations await this pair. These two are a natural hit.

Ox, Snake, Rooster
(Endurance, Accumulation, Application)

These conservative and consistent signs comprise the third harmonious trinity. These three soul mates conquer life through endurance, application, and a slow accumulation of energy. Although each sign is fixed and rigid in opinions and views, they are geniuses in the art of meticulous planning, and understand the wisdom of deferred gratification. Each one is a stable and long-lasting love partner ruled by deep, dark yin energy.

Ox—Snake

This combination is exemplified by a cozy fireside relationship between two karmic best friends. Each has a deep understanding of the other. There is excellent compatibility in friendship and in marriage for these two like-minded souls, and they tend to form unions of long duration. Slow and steady is how this couple approaches love and life.

Snake—Rooster

This is a winning combination of wisdom and work. The philosophical Snake and the industrious Rooster speak a common language of emotion, method, and fine physical appearance. Both are controlled, calculating, and industrious; however, the Rooster is busier, more efficient, and more aggressive than the contemplative Snake. Also, the Rooster is an early riser, while the Snake prefers to languish until noon.

Rooster—Ox

The Ox and the Rooster are the best of friends, and each enjoys the company of the other. Whether it's an Ox woman keeping the home fires burning for her sergeant major Rooster husband, or a male Ox enjoying his "little firecracker" of a wife efficiently running their home, this is a match destined to last. Mutual support and dedication to a cause or goal keep these two harmoniously in sync.

Rabbit, Goat, Pig
(Detachment, Propriety, Resignation)

These peaceful, empathetic signs comprise the fourth harmonious trinity. These three signs are artistic, refined, and well-mannered, and they share their quest for beauty in this life. They desire the preliminaries in romance and are the fine artists of lovemaking. Possessing more placid temperaments than the other nine signs, each one recoils and detaches from strife and ugliness. Their receptive, reflective yin energy seeks a gentle yet dominant lover.

Rabbit—Goat

The Rabbit and the Goat form a melodious union and exist in a world of aesthetics, culture, and refinement. These two best friends speak a similar language of art and creativity, and walk hand in hand in their quest to find and create beauty. Delicate and brittle emotionally, the Rabbit appreciates the Goat's awesome talent and world of fantasy. Both Rabbits and Goats start to become alive once the sun sets. The Goat is always late but worth the wait.

Goat—Pig

A loving relationship of courtesy and respect exists between these two gentle souls. The Goat teaches the Pig about romance, and in turn learns temperance from the Pig. Both are good Samaritans and casually take life as it comes. Living a serene and happy life is their goal, and both are deeply rooted in home and family.

Pig—Rabbit

This is a sweet relationship between two gentle souls. Both are well-mannered and genuinely virtuous. The diplomatic and socially adept Rabbit aids and befriends the shy Pig, to the benefit of both. These two are extremely good partners, share similar interests, and offer each other a quiet companionship and joy. A stimulating and satisfying partnership.

CHAPTER 5

鼠牛虎兔龍蛇馬羊猴鷄犬猪

LOVERS IN KIND

"LOVERS IN KIND" ARE TWO LOVERS who team up to complete one of the six life "palaces," and form unions that have a specific purpose and strong friendship component. Similar to the soul mates and trines, these combinations come together to complete an important task or project within the realm of the palace they occupy. Each sign is coupled together with the sign found directly after it. The six in kind palaces are:

* Creativity—Rat/Ox
* Accomplishment—Tiger/Rabbit
* Esoteric pursuit—Dragon/Snake
* Sexuality—Horse/Goat
* Trade/profession—Monkey/Rooster
* Family—Dog/Pig

Palace #1 Creative Expression— Rat (Begins), Ox (Completes)

Not only are the Rat and the Ox soul mates, but they also make up the life palace of creativity and artistic expression. These two souls are reverse sides of the same coin and form a mutual admiration society. The Rat and

Ox create together, and both are family- and security-oriented. They work together in love and in life, and each can remain devoted to the other for life. The Rat is so sentimental, and so vulnerable in love, that they can sacrifice everything on love's altar. Nothing is too good or costly for their beloved Ox.

Palace #2 Accomplishment/Forward Progress— Tiger (Force), Rabbit (Persuasion)

The Tiger's energy level and verve tends to overwhelm the Rabbit. The Tiger is boisterous, while the Rabbit is understated and artistic. The Tiger is as fearless as the Rabbit is timorous, and while there are much better matches for each of these two, they are brought together to grow and progress. Rabbits make their way in life by means of negotiation, diplomacy, and tact, while Tigers push past life's obstacles with sheer will and brute force. Both share the Wood element of expansion and rapid growth.

Palace #3 Esoteric Pursuit/Spirituality— Dragon (Illusionist, Magician) Snake (Sage)

The Dragon and the Snake make up the life palace of spirituality. The magic Dragon and mystic Snake are brought together to develop their "otherworldly" side. The relationship has the potential for happiness if the possessive Snake will allow the autonomous Dragon to leave the lair from time to time. However, if the Snake constricts the Dragon's movements, there could be friction. Infidelity can also become an issue between these two. However, together they learn to rise above the mundane and soar to new esoteric heights.

Palace #4 Sexuality/Reproduction— Horse (Yang Masculine) Goat (Yin Feminine)

Not only are the Horse and the Goat soul mates, but they are also lovers in kind. Together they comprise the life palace of sexuality. These two are opposite sides of the same coin and form a powerful combination of male and female essence. They compliment each other perfectly, with the Horse being the personification of the positive, yang day-force, and the Goat representing the absolute essence of the negative, yin night-force. Together these two make one perfect whole.

Palace #5 Trade/Profession— Monkey (Versatility) Rooster (Efficiency)

The Monkey and the Rooster are lovers in kind, and make up the life palace of career and profession. Monkeys advance their position through dexterity, while Roosters promote their interests via competence. Both share the Metal element of rigidity and structure hidden within their animal branches. This is a pairing that can bring rewards to both sides, especially in the realm of business. These two can become very successful together, either for the short term or for a lifetime.

Palace #6 Family/Home and Hearth— Dog (Creates) Pig (Finishes)

While they are not found in the traditional triangles of compatibility, the Dog and Pig are lovers in kind—*like* kind, that is. Together they make up the life palace of home and family, and they are brought together to develop their family side. With this team, one builds and the other furnishes—the earnest Dog lays the foundation and the affectionate Pig puts on the roof (so to speak). This pairing makes a loyal and romantic allegiance that is able to stand the test of time. Dogs and Pigs often celebrate golden wedding anniversaries.

CHAPTER 6

鼠牛虎兔龍蛇馬羊猴鷄犬猪

LOVERS RESOLVING KARMA

RELATIONSHIP DYNAMICS ARE DESTINED to be repeated until they are finally healed or "made right." "Lovers resolving karma" are two souls who meet up once again, this time in a new arena, in order to learn, reverse roles, and/or generally resolve past issues. These often tumultuous couplings can be identified by two animal signs (or years) between the individuals' birthdates. These particular connections are often of the "love-hate" variety and can make the partners feel like captives in their own arena.

Lovers resolving karma look good on paper, but something doesn't feel quite right to the lovers themselves. When two lovers find themselves in this pattern, it is a good bet that there are issues to resolve. Balance through tension is prevalent in these particular connections.

Parent-child relationships, as well as in-law and relative connections, can also be found within this relationship energy.

Lovers resolving karma are:

* Rat—Rabbit
* Ox—Dragon
* Tiger—Snake
* Rabbit—Horse

* Dragon—Goat
* Snake—Monkey
* Horse—Rooster
* Goat—Dog
* Monkey—Pig
* Rooster—Rat
* Dog—Ox
* Pig—Tiger

Here are a few examples:

* Rabbit male with Rat mother chooses a series of Rat females totally unsuited for him.
* Snake male with Tiger mother chooses stormy relationships with Tiger lovers in order to finally come to terms with his past.
* Pig female with philandering Monkey father chooses flirtatious Monkey man as husband. Same issues abound.

Rat—Rabbit

A Rat soul cannot live without intimate conversation, and the private Rabbit can leave the Rat feeling locked out and afloat. The Rabbit is not as invested in the relationship as her Rat partner, who wants to merge with the Rabbit completely. The Rabbit is also perceived as emotionally unavailable to the hypersensitive Rat, who in turn tends to view the Rabbit as a trophy or an acquisition of sorts. Being meticulous and at times overly concerned with her own health, the Rabbit finds the Rat's penchant for hypochondria and excesses in various health vices exasperating. In this situation, the Rat is not above feigning illness or fragility in order to get needed attention. Both share a love of the fine arts and socializing; however, due to their divergent dispositions, this pairing makes better friends than lovers.

Ox—Dragon

A clash of wills could derail this relationship, which makes well-defined roles for both parties critical. The key to a warm and enduring union is the Dragon spending more time at home. Both the Dragon and Ox need admiration, but it may not be forthcoming from either. The most serious obstacle facing this couple is the Dragon's penchant for love affairs. Infidelity in any form is unforgivable to the grounded Ox. When the choleric Ox becomes green with jealousy she sees only red, and neither matador nor musician can sooth this savage beast. The Dragon is an ethereal creature who rules the cosmos, but can easily feel trapped with little room to maneuver by the earthbound and dispassionate Ox.

Tiger—Snake

The action-oriented Tiger quickly becomes exasperated with the Snake's slow deliberations in life. Tigers move fast, think fast, and intend to cross life's finish line first. The Snake likes to calculate and ponder the meaning of life, which annoys the Tiger to no end. Because of this, the Snake often feels pushed and prodded, while the Tiger feels frustrated. The Snake carefully takes his time in everything he does, but the brusque Tiger perceives this trait as laziness. In relationships, these two may eventually go their separate ways or live autonomous lives. The Snake is the deliberating philosophizer who chafes against the Tiger's active lifestyle. The Tiger is of the opinion that the Snake "thinks too much" and should have more tangible projects to attend to. There are control issues here that will need to be resolved.

Horse—Rooster

This can be a difficult pairing of energies as the Rooster's fussiness can leave the Horse feeling tense and nervous. The Horse admires the Rooster, but in order to deal with the Rooster's verbal barbs and criticism he must learn to set limits and boundaries. Sparks can fly in any verbal battle that breaks out between them, and unfortunately neither partner feels a strong enough bond to make any sacrifices for the other. The superficial nature of this relationship means that the Horse and the Rooster make a better public than private couple. Attitude seems to be the primary issue between these two souls. This is a partnership that is either enchanting or totally unbearable.

Goat—Dog

A karmic power struggle if there ever was one! This double dose of cynicism does neither the pessimistic Dog nor the melancholy Goat any good. Both souls tend to look on the negative side of life and are prone to expect the worst. There are authority and control issues to be resolved here—and the sooner the better. The Dog herds the Goat into places he has no desire to be, thus bringing out his horns in defiance. Mutual expectations lead to disappointments, and more often than not it is the Dog who feels let down in this relationship. The Goat may feel compelled to live up to the Dog's unrealistic standards, while the Goat's attraction to drama stresses the Dog.

Monkey—Pig

Given the regularity with which these two souls come together, the natural assumption is that they are compatible. Unfortunately, they are only *familiar*, not compatible. Not only does this pair fall into the resolving karma, "we-have-issues" category, but the Monkey and the Pig are in a "karmic combatant" relationship with each other as well. Arguments due to different priorities regarding home and hearth can be troublesome. The Monkey has his own agenda, which may or may not include the Pig. Infidelities and indiscretions on the Monkey's part threaten to topple the Pollyanna Pig's world. The tricky Monkey just can't resist misleading the naive Pig, who stands to get hurt in this union.

CHAPTER 7

鼠牛虎兔龍蛇馬羊猴鷄犬猪

LOVERS IN OPPOSITION

WHILE FASCINATED BY AND INITIALLY ATTRACTED TO EACH OTHER, those signs in direct opposition eventually repel one another due to clashes in essential disposition. It is interesting to note that each of these oppositions is said to "open the money vault" for the other. Oppositional signs can be auspicious in business, each bringing to the table what the other lacks.

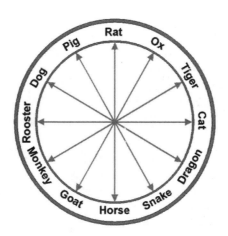

Rat—Horse

Interestingly, despite their opposition, these two souls meet up with each other frequently. Rat-year souls have a dual nature, exhibiting a need for security along with a need for independence. Rats need an understanding ear who will listen to their ideas, but the Horse is too preoccupied with his own dreams and ambitions. Love relationships in opposition seem initially to be "made in heaven" but can end in disappointment or bitterness. The Rat and the Horse are two out of the four "peach blossom" or love flower signs. Each is an incorrigible flirt and has a taste for sexual variety. The generous Horse can't abide the Rat's penny-pinching ways, and asking the Horse to sign a prenuptial agreement is akin to treason. This is a karmic opposition that makes better friends than lovers.

Ox—Goat

If one says black, the other says white. These two polarized opposites can make sparks fly with their radically different temperaments and opinions. Oxen are predictable and responsible, while Goats are artistic and completely unconcerned with time limits and tedious obligations. The Goat often experiences the Ox's sense of responsibility as overbearing and even tyrannical. In general, the Ox *acts* and the Goat *reacts* to life. This is a case of the motorcycle cop with the quota to meet versus the low-key, small-town sheriff who wants no confrontation. Oxen are regulated, organized, and controlled, while Goats are "loose cannons" that capriciously act and react in life. This is not an auspicious romantic combination, but other kinds of relationships such as siblings, business partners, and so on can be beneficial to both.

Tiger—Monkey

There can be a trust issue between these two polarized souls. The Tiger knows that the Monkey is capable of playing tricks and gaining confidences and this makes him nervous. The Tiger has no patience for the Monkey's schemes, tricks, or double-talk, and finds it difficult to tolerate the Monkey's "know-it-all" attitude. Then there's the matter of who is upstaging whom. There can only be one king or queen of the jungle, and the Tiger is it! Another problem between them is that the independent Tiger spends a lot of time away from home, which gives the Monkey too many opportunities to become involved in an affair. This pairing makes better accomplices in war, danger, or intrigue than it does in the lover's nest.

Rabbit—Rooster

No matter how hard these two try, compatibility seems beyond their reach. The brash Rooster's caustic criticism sets the Rabbit's nerves on edge. The Rooster considers the Rabbit the "weaker vessel," too delicate and easily hurt. If the Rabbit is a sexual submissive, the dominating Rooster may fit the bill, at least sexually. Outside of the bedroom, however, this is not an auspicious relationship. While relationships between *all* signs are possible, the combination of the aloof Rabbit and the cocky Rooster very rarely results in a long-term affair. At the relationship's best, the talented Rabbit can use the resourceful Rooster to help further or advance his career. At its worst, it can end with the Rabbit breaking things off to escape commitment, leaving the angry Rooster to stew in her own juice.

Dragon—Dog

This is an interesting relationship to say the least. Being polarized opposites, the Dragon and the Dog are as different as night and day. Because the traditional Dog clashes with the nontraditional Dragon, their relationship path is often filled with bumps and quagmires. The worst of these occur when the Dragon's brutally outspoken tendencies meet up with the Dog's thin emotional skin. Ouch! Another hurdle for this couple to overcome is the fact that the dutiful Dog does what is necessary while the Dragon does as he pleases. However, each possesses traits that the other would do well to learn. The Earth element that they share binds them somewhat, but they remain better colleagues than lovers. Possibly good business associates, but a difficult and complicated love union.

Snake—Pig

While both are agreeable and deeply feeling souls, the Snake and Pig are in direct opposition. They try to please each other but can't quite seem to make the connection. The honest Pig judges the Snake as having an "elastic," less-than-scrupulous conscience, which drives a wedge of tension between the two. In addition, the Pig has difficulty adhering to the Snake's penny-pinching ways, while the Snake is irritated by the Pig's over-indulgence in various material pleasures. One spends and the other saves, then abruptly, the Snake will turn extravagant while the Pig is financially circumspect. They just can't seem to get in sync with each other. For them to have any kind of a successful relationship, communication will be the key.

CHAPTER 8

鼠牛虎兔龍蛇馬羊猴雞犬豬

LOVERS LOCKED IN KARMIC COMBAT

"LOVERS LOCKED IN KARMIC COMBAT" are any two signs that are embroiled in unseen combat with one another. Amongst the couples suffering from this nasty karma are found previous enemies, rivals, and antagonists—the jailed meet their jailer, the duped meet their trickster, and each is wiser and experienced enough to do some reciprocal damage. These are the worst of the worst love combinations, so each is advised to steer psychically clear of the other. (Note: Those brave souls who strive to make amends and "fix" this cycle are functioning at a high spiritual level and are subconsciously balancing their karmic score card.) Choose your battles wisely here, as they could come back to haunt you.

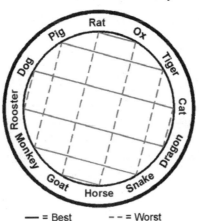

— = Best   - - - = Worst

Sometimes we place ourselves (or are placed) in these difficult energy patterns for personal spiritual growth. In the combatant vibration we can choose to conquer the animosity once and for all, or deal with it another time.

Rat—Goat

This relationship is a comedy of errors. The first obstacle they find is that the Rat is an early riser and the Goat is not. By the time the leisurely Goat wakes up to face the world, the energetic Rat has almost completed her day. In this pairing hyperactivity meets sloth, and the results can be inharmonious to say the least. The Rat is a thrifty and neat perfectionist while the Goat is a profuse shopper and less than tidy. These two have interests in common, but each views the world in such a radically different way that this pairing makes for difficult friendships, associates, and especially lovers.

Ox—Horse

The Horse would rather be any place except home. This is nothing less than treason to the Ox, who holds the family circle in such reverence. The Horse interprets the Ox's stability as dispassion. Neither sign has the foggiest idea of how the other thinks or feels. In Chinese folklore, it is said that the Horse and Ox can never share a stable. The Horse also doesn't appreciate being bossed around by the Ox, for whom taking charge comes naturally. Oxen prefer to spend their leisure time beautifying and improving their home, while Horses would rather be off at a concert, a play, a social event, or a sports activity. This disconnect makes for rivalries, poor romantic prospects, and difficult associations in general.

Tiger—Snake

Here we have a "double whammy" of karmic combatants, as well as two souls resolving karma (see Chapter 6). The Tiger and Snake have major differences of opinion on just about everything. In this relationship, the Snake feels pushed to go faster than he is comfortable with, while the Tiger tires of waiting for the Snake to make up his mind. The Tiger is externally focused while the Snake remains internally centered. The Snake's slow deliberations and endless pondering irritate the Tiger and make her impatient. Tigers move fast, think fast, and intend to cross life's finish line first.

The Snake takes his time in everything he does, and unfortunately the crass Tiger may label this trait as laziness.

Rabbit—Dragon

According to a Chinese proverb, "When the Rabbit comes, the Dragon's fortune goes." Thus there is a strong caution against this relationship. Unfortunately, the Rabbit and the Dragon are only one sign (and sometimes less than one year) apart, and therefore are often thrown together as classmates, colleagues, and spouses. The Rabbit is refined and mannerly, while the Dragon is crass and outspoken. This has the effect of creating many tensions. The Dragon overwhelms the Rabbit with her force of will and overbearing conduct. The Rabbit is discreet and courteous while the Dragon is direct and blunt, often revealing the Rabbit's secrets and causing him embarrassment. These two have such radically different temperaments that this pairing makes for almost insurmountable difficulties in friendships, family relations, and especially love relationships.

Monkey—Pig

Here we have another "double whammy" of two karmic combatants, as well as two souls resolving karma (see Chapter 6). The Monkey and Pig have major differences of opinion on just about everything. Considering the surprising regularity with which these two souls come together, the natural assumption would be that they are compatible. This is rarely the case, however. The Monkey has his own agenda, which may or may not include the Pig. The tricky Monkey just can't resist misleading the naive Pig, and the Pig is generally the last to find out about this. Unfortunately it is the Pig who stands to get hurt in this union.

Dog—Rooster

This combination is akin to a psychic blood fest. When the egotistic and sadistic Rooster teams up with the masochistic and insecure Dog, anything can happen. Each sign antagonizes the other, and the relationship is likely to bring out the worst in both personalities. This is a difficult combination of energies, as the thin-skinned Dog is not equipped to be the recipient of the Rooster's caustic verbal barbs. Should a full-fledged airing of grievances break out between these two, take cover! These two have such radically different temperaments and needs that this pairing makes for insurmountable difficulties between family members, work colleagues, and spouses.

The Steed and the Peach Blossom

In addition to the six major relationship energies covered previously, there are two more patterns that complete the eight karmic connections. These additional relationship energy patterns—the "steed" and the "peach blossom"—are challenging in a different way.

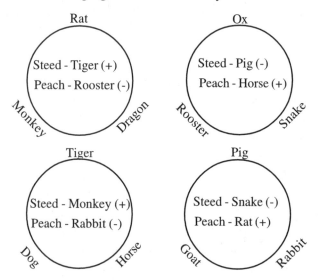

Each of the four compatibility trines or triangles—Rat/Dragon/Monkey, Ox/Snake/Rooster, Tiger/Horse/Dog, and Rabbit/Goat/Pig—have both a "steed" sign and a "peach blossom" sign in common. There are four "steed" signs: the Monkey, the Tiger, the Snake, and the Pig. They are also known as the four "Pegasus'" or "winged horses." These are the energies of movement, change, travel, and reevaluation. This movement can either be by choice (to walk in) or by force (to be pulled in).

Each of the four steed signs will pull the three signs connected to them into various kinds of activities. Sometimes these activities represent things that the partners have no desire to do (or no business doing). Examples of this dynamic would be a Monkey insistently demanding that their Tiger spouse take them home five minutes after arriving somewhere, or a Snake prodding a Goat colleague to invest in the latest "hot stock" financial scheme. As you can well imagine, the steed sign connections can be exhausting, draining, and depleting.

These connections *can* be positive if they urge resolution or usher in beneficial change. However, more often than not they are negative, especially if the sign connected to the steed feels coerced, overwhelmed, trapped, or otherwise pressured into unwanted action or change.

Each of the four compatibility groups shares a steed sign, and this sign will reveal where movement and change will occur. Expect things to shake up when:

* The Tiger/Horse/Dog pairs up with the Monkey.
* The Rabbit/Goat/Pig pairs up with the Snake.
* The Rat/Dragon/Monkey pairs up with the Tiger.
* The Ox/Snake/Rooster pairs up with the Pig.

The "peach blossom" signs are the Rat, Rabbit, Horse, and Rooster. These rascals are responsible for torrid love affairs and some memorable scenes. Everything from soul mates and twin flames to obsessions and fatal attractions are found in the peach blossom connections. If love drama is what you seek, look no further!

The peach blossoms are also known as the "love plums," "cherry blossoms," or simply "the flowers of love." These are the scandalous energies of which novels are written. In addition, these intense romance sparks can be the source either of celebration or of self-destruction: the choice lies entirely with the individuals involved. If you've ever obsessively wondered why you couldn't seem to disconnect from a distressing love affair, or why you were attracted to someone utterly unsuited for you, a peach blossom connection might have been the culprit.

Each of the four compatibility groups (triangles/trines) shares a peach blossom sign:

* The Rabbit is the peach to the Tiger/Horse/Dog.
* The Rat is the peach to the Rabbit/Goat/Pig.
* The Rooster is the peach to the Rat/Dragon/Monkey.
* The Horse is the peach to the Ox/Snake/Rooster.

An example of this ironic and tangled romantic mess might include a Dog who, against his better judgment, throws caution, good sense, and his present relationship to the wind for a Rabbit (the Dog's peach blossom), who in turn abandons said Dog for her own peach blossom—a Rat. The plot thickens as this same Rat becomes obsessed with a Rooster (the Rat's peach blossom) colleague at work, despite the possibility of jeopardizing his job. As you can see, the peach blossom connections have the potential of causing many sleepless nights, and are the relationships of which soap operas are made.

These connections can be even more complicated, as several of the peach blossom combinations also contain signs that fall into other categories. For example, two of the peach blossom connections fall into the "soul mate" vibration as well (see Chapter 3), such as the Dog with the Rabbit and the Dragon with the Rooster. Because they are both peach blossoms and soul mates to each other, they are at extremely high risk for obsessive love. Each can take the other to the top of life's mountain, or slay them face down in the valley of heartbreak.

Usually, the peach blossoms only cause some drama and memories for the rocking chair, but when peach blossoms/soul mates (Rabbit/Dog and Dragon/Rooster) part ways, the damage could be extensive, and neither may fully recover. Because of this double connection, these pairings carry the highest potential of becoming love-hate relationships.

Two more peach blossom connections fall into the double category, but this time the peach blossom is also the worst-of-the-worst "combatant." This occurs between the Rat and the Goat and between the Horse and the Ox. Because they are both peach blossoms they are easily attracted to each other, but as combatants they are at extremely high risk of broken love relationships that end on a sour note. Infatuated one minute, over it the next. When two peach blossoms/combatants separate (the Goat and the Rat or the Ox and the Horse), each breaths a sigh of relief and is glad to be free of the other.

Other peach blossom combinations, such as the Horse with the Rooster or the Snake, the Rat with the Rabbit or the Pig, the Rooster with the Rat or the Monkey, and the Rabbit with the Horse or the Tiger, can go their separate ways and leave on friendly terms.

CHAPTER 9

鼠牛虎兔龍蛇馬羊猴鶏犬猪

THE ELEMENTS OF CONNECTION— ARE YOU ELEMENTALLY COMPATIBLE?

IF YOU PLAYED THE CHILDHOOD GAME of "Rock, Paper, Scissors," you are already acquainted with the controlling/assisting cycles of the five Chinese Elements. The five Elements (Wood, Fire, Earth, Metal, and Water) both assist and control one another, thus preserving perfect balance in our universe. Indeed, the moment our souls entered our physical bodies at birth, they became in tune and in sync with the universal physics of matter. Not only do these basic Elemental influences shade and flavor our personalities, but they can be used as a potent compatibility meter, allowing us to have a glimpse into our connectedness. Do you and your partner help or hinder each other? Use the time-tested Elemental principles to see if you compliment or conflict with your lover. Do you bring happiness, wealth, and contentment to each other, or control, unwanted change, or even misfortune?

First, determine which Element ruled the year you were born from the following "earthly branches and heavenly stems" table. Next, ask yourself whether your birth-year animal branch is yin or yang. Remember, when the Wood Element is paired with a yin (-) sign (Ox, Rabbit, Snake, Goat, Rooster, Pig), it will always be "yin Wood" or "Yi." If the Wood Element is paired with a yang (+) sign (Rat, Tiger, Dragon, Horse, Monkey, Dog) it becomes "yang Wood" or "Jia." In this way, the five Elements become the 10 "heavenly stems."

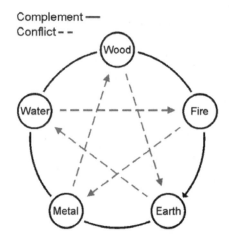

Complement —
Conflict - -

If you are a Fire Tiger, you are "yang Fire" or "Bing" because the Fire Element is paired with a yang branch animal sign. Similarly, if you are a Fire Ox, you are "yin Fire" or "Ding," as the Fire Element is paired with a yin branch animal sign. Here is an example: Mei Li was born on May 20, 1953—a Water Snake or "Gui Si" year—so she is yin (-) Water. Her partner, Li Chun, was born on October 5, 1956—a Fire Monkey or "Bing Shen" year—so he is yang (+) Fire. As her Water conquers and controls his Fire, he represents "entitled or earned wealth" for her. From his vantage point, her Water brings "beneficial change" to his life.

Earthly Branches and Heavenly Stems

Rat

1900 Jan 31 to Feb 18, 1901: + yang Metal Rat on the fence
1912 Feb 18 to Feb 5, 1913: + yang Water Rat on the mountain
1924 Feb 5 to Jan 24, 1925: + yang Wood Rat on the roof
1936 Jan 24 to Feb 10, 1937: + yang Fire Rat of the field
1948 Feb 10 to Jan 28, 1949: + yang Earth Rat of the granary
1960 Jan 28 to Feb 14, 1961: + yang Metal Rat on the crossbeams
1972 Feb 15 to Feb 2, 1973: + yang Water Rat on the hilltop
1984 Feb 2 to Feb 19, 1985: + yang Wood Rat of the mulberry tree
1996 Feb 19 to Feb 6, 1997: + yang Fire Rat of the grasslands
2008 Feb 7 to Jan 25, 2009 + yang Earth Rat of the granary

Ox

1901 Feb 19 to Feb 7, 1902: - yin Metal Ox on the road path
1913 Feb 6 to Jan 25, 1914: - yin Water Ox by the pond
1925 Jan 25 to Feb 12, 1926: - yin Wood Ox of the golden sea
1937 Feb 11 to Jan 30, 1938: - yin Fire Ox of the little Stream
1949 Jan 29 to Feb 16, 1950: - yin Earth Ox of the shelter
1961 Feb 15 to Feb 4, 1962: - yin Metal Ox on the road
1973 Feb 3 to Jan 22, 1974: - yin Water Ox of the little stream
1985 Feb 20 to Feb 8, 1986: - yin Wood Ox of the golden sea
1997 Feb 7 to Jan 27, 1998: - yin Fire Ox of the little stream
2009 Jan 26 to Feb 13, 2010: - yin Earth Ox of the shelter

Tiger

1902 Feb 8 to Jan 28, 1903: + yang Water Tiger of the stream
1914 Jan 26 to Feb 13, 1915: + yang Wood Tiger of forest
1926 Feb 13 to Feb 1, 1927: + yang Fire Tiger of the furnace
1938 Jan 31 to Feb 18, 1939: + yang Earth Tiger climbing mountain
1950 Feb 17 to Feb 5, 1951: + yang Metal Tiger of mountain pines
1962 Feb 5 to Jan 24, 1963: + yang Water Tiger of the stream
1974 Jan 23 to Feb 10, 1975: + yang Wood Tiger of the forest
1986 Feb 9 to Jan 28, 1987: + yang Fire Tiger of the furnace
1998 Jan 28 to Feb 15, 1999: + yang Earth Tiger climbing mountain
2010 Feb 14 to Feb 2, 2011: + yang Metal Tiger of mountain pines

Rabbit

1903 Jan 29 to Feb 15, 1904: - yin Water Rabbit of the forest pond
1915 Feb 14 to Feb 2, 1916: - yin Wood Rabbit of enlightenment
1927 Feb 2 to Jan 22, 1928: - yin Fire Rabbit dreaming of moon
1939 Feb 19 to Feb 7, 1940: - yin Earth Rabbit of pine mountains
1951 Feb 6 to Jan 26, 1952: - yin Metal Rabbit of the burrow
1963 Jan 25 to Feb 12, 1964: - yin Water Rabbit of the forest pond
1975 Feb 11 to Jan 30, 1976: - yin Wood Rabbit of enlightenment
1987 Jan 29 to Feb 16, 1988: - yin Fire Rabbit dreaming of moon
1999 Feb 16 to Feb 4, 2000: - yin Earth Rabbit of pine mountains
2011 Feb 3 to Jan 22, 2012: - yin Metal Rabbit of the burrow

Dragon

1904 Feb 16 to Feb 3, 1905: + yang Wood Dragon of the whirlpool
1916 Feb 3 to Jan 22, 1917: + yang Fire Dragon of the sky
1928 Jan 23 to Feb 9, 1929: + yang Earth Dragon of virtue
1940 Feb 8 to Jan 26, 1941: + yang Metal Dragon of patience
1952 Jan 27 to Feb 13, 1953: + yang Water Dragon of the rain
1964 Feb 13 to Feb 1, 1965: + yang Wood Dragon of the whirlpool
1976 Jan 31 to Feb 17, 1977: + yang Fire Dragon of the sky
1988 Feb 17 to Feb 5, 1989: + yang Earth Dragon of virtue
2000 Feb 5 to Jan 23, 2001: + yang Metal Dragon of patience
2012 Jan 23 to Feb 9, 2013: + yang Water Dragon of the rain

Snake

1905 Feb 4 to Jan 24, 1906: - yin Wood Snake of the forest trees
1917 Jan 23 to Feb 10, 1918: -yin Fire Snake of lamps
1929 Feb 10 to Jan 29, 1930: - yin Earth Snake of desert sands
1941 Jan 27 to Feb 14, 1942: - yin Metal Snake of molded bronze
1953 Feb 14 to Feb 2, 1954: - yin Water Snake of the wetlands
1965 Feb 2 to Jan 20, 1966: - yin Wood Snake of the forest trees
1977 Feb 18 to Feb 6, 1978: - yin Fire Snake of lamps
1989 Feb 6 to Jan 26, 1990: - yin Earth Snake of desert sands
2001 Jan 24 to Feb 11, 2002 - yin Metal Snake of molded bronze
2013 Feb 10 to Jan 30, 2014: - yin Water Snake of the wetlands

Horse

1906 Jan 25 to Feb 12, 1907: + yang Fire Horse of the celestial river (stars)
1918 Feb 11 to Jan 31, 1919: + yang Earth Horse of the stable
1930 Jan 30 to Feb 16, 1931: + yang Metal Horse of the palace
1942 Feb 15 to Feb 4, 1943: + yang Water Horse of battlefield
1954 Feb 3 to Jan 23, 1955: + yang Wood Horse of the clouds
1966 Jan 21 to Feb 8, 1967: + yang Fire Horse of the celestial river (stars)
1978 Feb 7 to Jan 27, 1979: + yang Earth Horse of the stable
1990 Jan 27 to Feb 14, 1991: + yang Metal Horse of the palace
2002 Feb 12 to Jan 31, 2003: + yang Water Horse of the battlefield
2014 Jan 31 to Feb 18, 2015: + yang Wood Horse of the clouds

Goat

1907 Feb 13 to Feb 1, 1908: - yin Fire Goat of the lost sheep
1919 Feb 1 to Feb 19, 1920: - yin Earth Goat of the pasture
1931 Feb 17 to Feb 5, 1932: - yin Metal Goat of the mines (fortune)
1943 Feb 5 to Jan 24, 1944: - yin Water Goat of the gathering flock
1955 Jan 24 to Feb 11, 1956: - yin Wood Goat of dedication
1967 Feb 9 to Jan 29, 1968: - yin Fire Goat of the lost sheep
1979 Jan 28 to Feb 15, 1980: - yin Earth Goat of the pasture
1991 Feb 15 to Feb 3, 1992: - yin Metal Goat of the mines (fortune)
2003 Feb 1 to Jan 21, 2004: - yin Water Goat of the gathering flock
2015 Feb 19 to Feb 7, 2016: - yin Wood Goat of dedication

Monkey

1908 Feb 2 to Jan 21, 1909: + yang Earth Monkey of independence
1920 Feb 20 to Feb 7, 1921: + yang Metal Monkey eating pomegranate
1932 Feb 6 to Jan 25, 1933: + yang Water Monkey of elegance
1944 Jan 25 to Feb 12, 1945: + yang Wood Monkey of the trees
1956 Feb 12 to Jan 30, 1957: + yang Fire Monkey of the foothills
1968 Jan 30 to Feb 16, 1969: + yang Earth Monkey of independence
1980 Feb 16 to Feb 4, 1981: + yang Metal Monkey eating pomegranate
1992 Feb 4 to Jan 22, 1993: + yang Water Monkey of elegance
2004 Jan 22 to Feb 8, 2005: + yang Wood Monkey of the trees
2016 Feb 8 to Jan 27, 2017: + yang Fire Monkey of the foothills

Rooster

1909 Jan 22 to Feb 9, 1910: - yin Earth Rooster of foraging
1921 Feb 8 to Jan 27, 1922: - yin Metal Rooster of steel cages
1933 Jan 26 to Feb 13, 1934: - yin Water Rooster of barnyard pond
1945 Feb 13 to Feb 1, 1946: - yin Wood Rooster crowing at dawn
1957 Jan 31 to Feb 17, 1958: - yin Fire Rooster of seclusion
1969 Feb 17 to Feb 5, 1970: - yin Earth Rooster of foraging
1981 Feb 5 to Jan 24, 1982: - yin Metal Rooster of steel cages
1993 Jan 23 to Feb 9, 1994: - yin Water Rooster of barnyard pond
2005 Feb 9 to Jan 28, 2006: - yin Wood Rooster crowing at dawn
2017 Jan 28 to Feb 15, 2018: - yin Fire Rooster of seclusion

Dog

1910 Feb 10 to Jan 29, 1911: + yang Metal Dog of gold bracelets
1922 Jan 28 to Feb 15, 1923: + yang Water Dog of deep oceans
1934 Feb 14 to Feb 3, 1935: + yang Wood Dog on guard
1946 Feb 2 to Jan 21, 1947: + yang Fire Dog of dreams (sleep)
1958 Feb 18 to Feb 7, 1959: + yang Earth Dog of the mountain
1970 Feb 6 to Jan 26, 1971: + yang Metal Dog of gold bracelets
1982 Jan 25 to Feb 12, 1983: + yang Water Dog of deep oceans
1994 Feb 10 to Jan 30, 1995: + yang Wood Dog on guard
2006 Jan 29 to Feb 17, 2007: + yang Fire Dog of dreams (sleep)
2018 Feb 16 to Feb 4, 2019: + yang Earth Dog of the mountain

Pig

1911 Jan 30 to Feb 17, 1912: - yin Metal Pig of jewelry
1923 Feb 16 to Feb 4, 1924: - yin Water Pig of the wide sea
1935 Feb 4 to Jan 23, 1936: - yin Wood Pig of travel and journeys
1947 Jan 22 to Feb 9, 1948: - yin Fire Pig cresting the mountain
1959 Feb 8 to Jan 27, 1960: - yin Earth Pig of the monastery
1971 Jan 27 to Jan 15, 1972: - yin Metal Pig of jewelry
1983 Feb 13 to Feb 1, 1984: - yin Water Pig of the wide sea
1995 Jan 31 to Feb 18, 1996: - yin Wood Pig of travel and journeys
2007 Feb 18 to Feb 6, 2008: - yin Fire Pig cresting the mountain
2019 Feb 5 to Jan 24, 2020: - yin Earth Pig of the monastery

Now, find your birth Element, and then look to that Element's description to see how it will influence your relationships.

Wood

The Wood Element expresses imagination, creativity, simplicity, idealism, and compassion. It also represents the family and artistic theory. Similar to the great Sequoia tree, the nature of Wood is to move upward toward the light, to spread outward and expand. Its creative nature is naturally drawn to the arts, to aesthetic pursuits, and to beauty in general. Wood Element people have high-minded values and believe in the dignity of every human being. The Wood Element also brings cooperation, so people born under this element understand the value of teamwork and excel in organizing large projects. They are also progressive thinkers and far-sighted in their goals and ventures. The Wood Element endows each sign with a natural presence and sense of propriety; however, Wood is also incendiary and capable of producing a combustible temper. If you were born into a Wood year:

* Your sexual style is experimental and casual.

* Your predominant sense is touch.

* You assist/help partners born into Fire years.

* You are assisted by partners born into Water years.

* Your traits are kindness, generosity, and expansion, but also anger, frustration, and depression.

If you are yang Wood "Jia" (Wood Rat, Wood Tiger, Wood Dragon, Wood Horse, Wood Monkey, or Wood Dog):

* Sudden wealth—yang Earth Wu

* Entitled wealth—yin Earth Ji

* Resources/contentment—yin Water Gui

* Controller/positive change—yin Metal Xin

* Controller/unfavorable conflict—yang Metal Geng

If you are yin Wood "Yi" (Wood Ox, Wood Rabbit, Wood Snake, Wood Goat, Wood Rooster, or Wood Pig):

* Sudden wealth—yin Earth Ji

* Entitled wealth—yang Earth Wu

* Resources/contentment—yang Water Ren

* Controller/positive change—yang Metal Geng

* Controller/unfavorable conflict—yin Metal Xin

Wood Element Combinations

The Wood Rat is diligent, successful, and blessed with a curious and inquisitive mind. The youthful, forward-moving Rat loves to find out how things work. This is a social and friendly soul, but the Wood Rat may have trouble with intimacy and experience a tumultuous love life. Agreeable and thoughtful of others, they seek acknowledgment and approval. Wood Rats seek security and will always plan for their future.

The Wood Ox possesses authority and natural presence. Their relentless determination assures them of success in life. This is the most artistic of the Oxen, and is oftentimes blessed with profound mechanical aptitude. Music, creative writing, and poetry all come naturally to the Wood Ox. A natural leader and authority, this soul may encounter rivalries and jealousies from less talented individuals.

The Wood Tiger is a more sedate personality who isn't as impetuous as other Tigers, preferring instead to look before she leaps. Impartial and a good judge of character, Wood Tigers are intellectual and understand the importance of a team effort. Group efforts bring them great popularity. Wood Tigers will have a diverse selection of friends, some from unusual or eccentric lifestyles. Moving ever upward, the Wood Tiger outgrows positions and changes professions frequently.

The Wood Rabbit possesses poetic gifts and is attracted to the fine arts. Gardening and landscaping will please their sense of beauty and harmony while fulfilling their need for space and freedom. The Wood Rabbit is an outwardly shy, highly intuitive, and deep-feeling soul. This is the gentle seducer who avoids restraints and obligations. Wood Rabbits are collectors of art, antiques, and other objects of beauty.

The Wood Dragon is imaginative and talented, and able to improvise when faced with chaotic and unexpected events. This Dragon possesses the gift of creative invention and is attracted to nature and symbols of beauty. Dynamic and courageous, yet seductive and seeking to please, the Wood Dragon has a duel nature. More practical and moderate than their other Dragon counterparts, Wood Dragons have their feet firmly planted on the ground, and they are much less prone to have a heated temper.

The Wood Snake craves quiet, stability, and plenty of privacy. This is a sympathetic and earnest Snake, who shares philosophical ideas with all who care to listen. This Snake has a strong need for independence and can successfully take on large projects. The aesthetic nature of Wood blesses this Snake with a love of culture and the fine arts. Wood Snakes are possessive and are very protective of their home and family.

The Wood Horse has a quick and disciplined mind, and is a cheerful and cooperative team player. As progressive and modern thinkers, changes and new innovations capture their vivid imagination. The most social of all the Horse Element combinations, Wood Horses are amusing and adept conversationalists, and tend to be attracted to the theater and public speaking, as well as to sports and athletics.

The **Wood Goat** tends to worry more than other Goats. On the upside, they are romantic, acquiescing, generous, and well-liked. This is a courteous Goat with a good sense of humor. The Wood Goats are the most sentimental of the Goat Element combination, and are eager to please the ones they love. This is a nurturing Goat who has a soft heart toward stray animals and compassion for friends down on their luck. Wood Goats can always be found giving freely of their resources.

The **Wood Monkey** is resourceful and enthusiastic but may have trouble slowing down or pacing him/her self. This Monkey maintains high standards for themselves as well as others. They are gregarious, socially adept, and possess a quick-witted sense of humor. Personal expression is essential to the Wood Monkey, and because of this they are active participants in life. Their curious mind excels at solving difficult problems and they are never without resources.

The **Wood Rooster** is more thoughtful and tactful than the other Rooster Element combinations. They are open-minded, ambitious, and happiest amongst a social group sharing lively conversation. Wood Roosters are also passionate—just as Wood can incinerate, they are susceptible to excesses at times. They must use their clear-sightedness to avoid getting carried away or pushed to excessive anger. The Wood Rooster gains equilibrium and self-assurance closer to midlife.

The **Wood Dog** is affectionate and youthful, and known for having strong convictions. This is the "team player" of the Dog Element combinations. Idealistic and eager to learn, the Wood Dog is popular and forms intimate bonds with others. This is a charming, personable soul who defends his/her values with tenacity and tact. Watchful and nurturing, Wood Dogs can organize major projects and manage large groups of people with ease.

The **Wood Pig** is a well-balanced and charming soul who loves to be close to nature, the woods, and the earth. The Wood Element plays the role of "muse" for this Pig, who may very well express themselves through the arts. Possessing uncanny intuition and influence, the Wood Pig is passionate, bawdy, and cannot live without physical love. The Wood Element may also incline this Pig to commit excesses with both food and drink.

Fire

The Fire Element expresses dynamic passion, energy, aggression, and leadership. The nature of Fire is to arouse, change, convert, consume, resolve, and bring about an outcome. The Fire Element will tend to multiply each sign's inborn talents and energies. Fire Element people have the gifts of leadership, passion, and assertiveness. Decisive and masterful, those born into the Fire Element rarely have trouble making decisions, and they attract others with their strong and radiant personalities. Fire Element souls have an abundance of energy that produces impatience. The movement of Fire is rapid and can consume one's energies if it is not balanced with relaxation and moderation. The Fire Element represents the ability to be decisive, to lead, and to act spontaneously without forethought. Fire punctuates each sign with an exclamation mark!

If you were born into a Fire year:

* Your sexual style is dominant and/or sadistic.

* Your predominant sense is sight.

* You assist/help partners born into Earth years.

* You are assisted by partners born into Wood years.

* Your dominant traits include joy, leadership, sincerity, and respect, but also impatience, arrogance, and haste.

If you are yang Fire "Bing" (Fire Rat, Fire Tiger, Fire Dragon, Fire Horse, Fire Monkey, or Fire Dog):

* Sudden wealth—yang Metal Geng

* Entitled wealth—yin Metal Xin

* Resources/contentment—yin Wood Yi

* Controller/positive change—yin Water Gui

* Controller/unfavorable conflict—yang Water Ren

If you are yin Fire "Ding" (Fire Ox, Fire Rabbit, Fire Snake, Fire Goat, Fire Rooster, or Fire Pig):

* Sudden wealth—yin Metal Xin

* Entitled wealth—yang Metal Geng

* Resources/contentment—yang Wood Jia

* Controller/positive change—yang Water Ren

* Controller/unfavorable conflict—yin Water Gui

Fire Element Combinations

The Fire Rat is determined and self-disciplined, and more aggressive by nature than the other Rat Element combinations. They are enthusiastic regarding their projects and must guard against overwork. This is a soul of strong moral principles and high-minded thinking. This eternal student absorbs knowledge like a sponge and is well-versed in a wide variety of subjects. A lover of travel and fashionable clothes, the Fire Rat is the most generous of the Rats and, interestingly, the most capable of leadership.

The Fire Ox is talented with his hands and highly creative. The Fire Ox has tremendous energy, which can make him impatient to reach his goals. This Ox must respect his body's limits and guard against exhaustion. The Fire Ox is a conqueror and may be drawn to politics or perhaps even the military. Despite this, they remain fiercely individualistic. Fire Oxen are very family-oriented and are always king or queen of their castle.

The Fire Tiger has been blessed with extraordinary leadership aptitude. Fire Tigers are volatile and passionate in life and in love. Patience isn't their strong point, so the Fire Tiger may find it hard to delay gratification. Always up for a new adventure, the Fire Tiger is action-oriented, extravagant, and expressive. Rather nomadic by nature, Fire Tigers enjoy frequent changes of environment and are rarely content staying anywhere for too long. These are the most independent members of the Tiger's pride.

The Fire Rabbit is more high-spirited and stubborn than other Rabbit Element combinations. They personify the Rabbit essence of "detachment." The Fire Rabbit will have a tendency to keep her distance, especially when feeling rejected or excluded. The Fire Element releases a boldness that will overcome the Rabbit's natural reticence. More outspoken than other Rabbit Element combinations, the Fire Rabbit has an inner flame that strengthens her courage and adds aggression.

The Fire Dragon is more ambitious than other Dragon Element combinations. Articulate in speech and blessed with a tremendous desire to succeed, Fire Dragons are hard workers, natural thespians, and born leaders. The Fire Dragon is admired for her integrity and forthright manner. The most strong-willed of the Dragons, they tend to rely on their own judgment without taking into account others' views. Always in search of admiration, the Fire Dragon finds it difficult to embrace humility.

The Fire Snake is more decisive and self-assured than other Snake Element combinations. They are natural leaders—healthy, vital, ambitious, and confident. They are also tough enough to get the job done. The Fire Snake tends to be more forceful, outgoing, and energetic than some of the other Snakes, but remains compassionate and deep thinking. This Snake wins respect and support with his firm and persistent manner. They possess an excellent sense of humor and have a wide circle of friends.

The Fire Horse will make her mark early in life and exhibit her various talents in astonishing ways. The soul born under this influence will be endowed with superior wisdom, but perseverance may be difficult. Fire Horses display above-average qualities of leadership and draw others to their warmth and brilliance. Both the positive and negative characteristics of the Fire Horse will be multiplied tenfold, as this is the most ardent and impetuous of Horse Element combinations.

The Fire Goat is a strong personality. Blessed with extraordinary artistic talents, this Goat is a natural writer, poet, and artisan, and is generally much more expressive than other Goat Element combinations. Generous and charismatic, the Fire Goat inspires others and is one of the only Goats aggressive enough to be a leader. They are extroverted and charming, but they are also self-indulgent and manipulative.

The Fire Monkey is competitive and popular. Having wide and diverse interests, this energetic and animated Monkey is a problem solver and a self-starter. Fire Monkeys are creative, resourceful, and highly competitive. The Fire Element imparts great vitality and good health, but could also consume much of their energy. Their fertile imagination produces an ingenious, albeit suspicious, personality.

The Fire Rooster is intense, energetic, and a natural leader. This lively Rooster has difficulty staying on one subject and thus can have many projects in the works. The Fire Rooster is self-assured and determined, as well as expressive and brutally candid with their observations. The Fire Element imparts great vitality and a highly competitive nature. Mercurial, zealous, and suspicious of others' motives, this is the most strong-willed of the Rooster Element combinations.

The Fire Dog is dynamic and connects easily with others. They are opinionated, dynamic, and radiant with energy. Highly animated and out-spoken, Fire Dogs have no problem expressing themselves, and many choose to go into politics or the entertainment industry. The Fire Dog has an alluring and friendly personality that conceals a self-effacing and anx-ious spirit. Possessing great charm, the Fire Dog stands her ground and is fierce only when diplomacy has failed.

The Fire Pig is decisive and more self-assured than other Pig Element combinations. This is an alluring soul—opinionated, adventuresome, and radiant with energy. The Fire Pig is most fortunate financially, due to his com-bination of ambition and purity of heart. Fire bestows leadership abilities and bravery to this soul, and the Fire Pig often chooses to be a "first-responder" by profession. Many are firemen, police officers, and emergency workers.

Earth

The Earth Element expresses stability, reliability, practicality, and common sense. The nature of Earth is to "ground," to keep whole, and to preserve. The Earth Element is symbolic of the mother's protected womb of peace and safety. Those born under the Earth Element are both practical and industrious. They have exceptional powers of organization and are competent masterminds and executives. Honest, serious, and conservative, Earth Element people are capable of making wise decisions.

If you were born under the Earth Element:

* Your sexual style is self-indulgent and excessive.

* Your predominant sense is smell.

* You assist/help partners born into Metal years.

* You are assisted by partners born into Fire years.

* Your dominant traits are fairness, sympathy, and centeredness, but also obsession and worry.

If you are yang Earth "Wu" (Earth Rat, Earth Tiger, Earth Dragon, Earth Horse, Earth Monkey, or Earth Dog):

* Sudden wealth—yang Water Ren

* Entitled wealth—yin Water Gui

* Resources/contentment—yin Fire Ding

* Controller/positive change—yin Wood Yi

* Controller/unfavorable conflict—yang Wood Jia

If you are Yin Earth "Ji" (Earth Ox, Earth Rabbit, Earth Snake, Earth Goat, Earth Rooster, Earth Pig):

* Sudden wealth—yin Water Gui

* Entitled wealth—yang Water Ren

* Resources/contentment—yang Fire Bing

* Controller/positive change—yang Wood Jia

* Controller/unfavorable conflict—yin Wood Yi

Earth Element Combinations

The Earth Rat is sensible and alert. He has remarkable willpower but also has a tendency to worry about security and finances. The Earth Element tempers the high-strung Rat personality and provides a nurturing, down-to-earth temperament. The Earth Element also makes this Rat prudent, crafty, and subtle. Earth Rats need constant activity to keep them from dwelling on or becoming mired in their own problems.

The Earth Ox is the most loyal and steadfast of the Ox family. Stoic on the outside yet vulnerable on the inside, the Earth Ox is a deep thinker and tends to be a loner. Food and the earth itself serve as a refuge that entices the Earth Ox to close the door on the human race and pursue meditation, relaxation, and solitude. Enduring and persistent, this is the slowest but surest of all the Oxen.

The Earth Tiger looks for practicality in everything she undertakes. The Earth Tiger is not as hot-headed as other Tigers, and possesses a more mature temperament. The Earth Tiger nurtures small helpless things like babies, stray animals, and sad friends down on their luck. They are deeply conscientious and humanitarian in spirit. A fair-minded leader, the Earth Tiger makes an excellent counselor and judge.

The Earth Rabbit has excellent deductive powers and prefers solid and reliable pursuits. The Earth Element endows her with more foresight and capacity for organization. This is the most conservative of the Rabbit element combinations. Earth Rabbits are wise and sensible with financial matters. They are also quiet, critical, serious, introverted, and respected. This is the consummate diplomat and peacemaker.

The Earth Dragon is more realistic than other Dragons but does enjoy speculation and the accumulation of wealth. A conscientious and hard worker, the Earth Dragon takes on chores and problems which others find impossible to conquer. Prudent yet suspicious, the Earth Dragon has eyes in the back of his head and misses nothing. This is the most nurturing soul of the Dragon family—always willing to help out in a crisis and fiercely protective of family and loved ones.

The Earth Snake is a secure and cozy Snake who loves elegance and the material comforts in life. With an ability to turn inward and retreat from the outside world, the Earth Snake is relaxed and at times lethargic. They are prone to "hibernation," with many choosing a reclusive life of spirituality and contemplation. The dreamy, stay-at-home Snake is often sought out for her wise council.

The Earth Horse is careful, capable, and sensible. Horses born under this influence are methodical in manner, excellent managers, and reinforce solid foundations in all that they do. Conservative by nature, the Earth Horse is a realist who knows how to advance prudently and skeptically. This is a less ambitious yet more meticulous Horse who has a tendency to be possessive and very security conscious.

The Earth Goat is sympathetic, honest, and well-liked. Financially fortunate, the Earth Goat has a taste for luxury and the finer things in life. The most suspicious and mistrustful Goat Element combination, the Earth Goat exhibits unpredictable moods and mental processes. The Earth Goat isn't as outgoing as the other Goats, and friendships must stand the test of time. This artistic and deep thinking soul of the Goat family lives in a world of dreams and fantasy.

The Earth Monkey is well-informed, benevolent, and kind. They can be cursed with perfectionist ways and are more pragmatic and realistic than other Monkeys. Most of their enterprises are motivated by their acquisitive nature and a desire for increasing possessions. This Monkey likes activities that will bear fruit, and tends to be attracted to speculation, sales, and real estate. Although they can be fearful about the future, Earth Monkeys are blessed with financial intuition and good monetary instincts.

The Earth Rooster has a profound perspective on life and is the most persistent and persevering of the Rooster Element combinations. This Rooster does not like to take risks and has the ability to build upon the previous work of others. Success, security, and appearance are important elements in the life of the Earth Rooster. Earth Roosters are realistic, pragmatic, and shrewd, and tend to bury their treasures safely away.

The Earth Dog possesses a powerful need for recognition and appreciation. Independent and gifted, they are capable of devoting themselves totally to a cause or to achieving social ambitions. The Earth Dog is long-suffering in love, and can easily be taken advantage of due to his overly generous nature. Earth Dogs jealously protect their home and loved ones. They are fiercely proud, but can always be counted on to be fair and impartial mediators.

The Earth Pig is shrewd and imaginative, but perfectly realistic and materialistic. Earth Pigs are strong and self-confident, and enjoy socializing with their inner circle of trusted friends. This artistic Pig may express her creativity via practical and pragmatic avenues such as computers and logic systems. This combination of sign and Element creates a soul who appears to be submissive, but who is in fact completely in control from behind the scenes.

Metal

The Metal Element expresses structure, fixed values, strength of will, and fluency of speech. The nature of Metal is to define and to strengthen.

The Metal Element symbolizes clear thinking, sincerity, and accuracy. Metal Element people have the gift of structure and the ability to interface easily with the outside world. Those born into the Metal Element set and follow their own goals with fervor and passion. Metal is determined and fixed, holding each sign in a position of strength by serving as a foundation and base.

The Metal Element will also add rigidity to a sign. Because this is a fixed Element, it can contribute a certain stubbornness and reluctance to compromise. As the Metal Element represents strength of will and fluency of speech, people born under this Element tend to speak freely, candidly, and even bluntly. Metal Element souls are fiercely independent, solitary, and blessed with perseverance.

If you were born under the Metal Element:

* Your sexual style is perverted and rigid.

* Your predominant sense is taste.

* You assist/heip partners born into Water years.

* You are assisted by partners born into Earth years.

* Your dominant traits are virtuousness, structure, and clarity, but also narcissism, melancholy, and rigidity.

If you are yang Metal "Geng" (Metal Rat, Metal Tiger, Metal Dragon, Metal Horse, Metal Monkey, or Metal Dog):

* Sudden wealth—yang Wood Jia

* Entitled wealth—yin Wood Yi

* Resources/contentment—yin Earth Ji

* Controller/positive change—yin Fire Ding

* Controller/unfavorable conflict—yang Fire Bing

If you are yin Metal "Xin" (Metal Ox, Metal Rabbit, Metal Snake, Metal Goat, Metal Rooster, or Metal Pig):

* Sudden wealth—yin Wood Yi

* Entitled Wealth—yang Wood Jia

* Resources/Contentment—yang Earth Wu

* Controller/Positive Change—yang Fire Bing

* Controller/Unfavorable Conflict—yin Fire Ding

Metal Element Combinations

The Metal Rat is extremely emotional, a shrewd socialite, and knows how to use the system to get ahead. The Metal Rat can be rigid and adamant in expressing his opinions. Argumentative when provoked, this Rat has a sharp tongue and is capable of verbally shredding an opponent. This Rat is very success-oriented, with strong monetary instincts and the ability to save for a rainy day.

The Metal Ox can be rigid and even severe at times. Metal Oxen are ambitious, success-oriented, and unwavering in determination. This strong combination of sign and Element is dutiful and determined, undaunted by hardships, drawbacks, or initial failures. Metal Oxen are financially fortunate, constant, and true to their word. They can make an articulate moral arbitrator or judge.

The Metal Tiger is glamorous and distinctive in appearance. This Tiger has much ambition and is fascinating to those around her. Although goals may change from time to time, the Metal Element bestows perseverance to this Tiger. Metal Tigers will be unbending as well as daring in expression. For greatest success, the Metal Tiger must be able to compromise with those who are in a position to benefit her.

The Metal Rabbit is clever and sly, with much artistic ability, acute intelligence, and a deeply romantic core. This is a "solitary" Element, intensifying the Rabbit's need for privacy and their lone-wolf-style of problem-solving. The Metal Rabbit must learn which battles to lose in order to win his wars. This Rabbit likes to mix in the best circles and usually has an intimate but very loyal group of friends. This is the most private of the Rabbits, not prone to compromise, and a soul who keeps his own council.

The Metal Dragon is capable and cunning, and particularly shrewd in business matters. This is due to the Metal Element contributing its good financial sense. Although argumentative and the most sharp-tongued of the Dragon family, Metal Dragons are natural-born leaders. They are also attracted to spiritual pursuits and tend to isolate themselves for periods of solitary contemplation. This is an energetic and decisive Dragon who excels at commanding others and facing confrontation.

The Metal Snake is cautious and skeptical. They keep their own counsel and prefer to work independently. They are capable of great profit and wealth, as strong financial instincts are present with this combination of sign and Element. The Metal Snake is blessed with acute intelligence and a deeply sensitive core. These souls have a tremendous ability to influence the outcomes of different situations. They are quiet and confident, and have a cultured appreciation of the fine arts, literature, and music.

The Metal Horse has a magnetic personality. Undeterred when it comes to career ambitions, this is the dynamic "cutting blade" of the Horse family. Effective and adept in her chosen area of interest, the Metal Horse does not hesitate to act quickly on a decision, and will readily take on a crusade or worthy cause. Just and honest, this Horse is an ardent idealist and humanitarian in nature, with very high standards for both herself and others.

The Metal Goat has the heart of a warrior beneath an easygoing exterior. More energetic and decisive than the other Goat Element combinations, these souls are not as harmless as they look. The Metal Goat is a perfectionist and has a tendency to be judgmental. They are a curious and contradictory mixture of compromise and stubbornness, dependence, and self-sufficiency. The influence of Metal on the Goat is light and easy in some situations, yet rigid and uncompromising in others.

The Metal Monkey is independent and astute. While they are determined souls, they can also become easily frustrated by failure and impatient with their life progress. Although they are attracted to metaphysics, Metal Monkeys tend to be rigid in their beliefs and not as social as other Monkeys. Experts at implementing plans, the Metal Monkey will strive for high positions. They are usually involved in the "nuts and bolts" of putting an idea together.

The Metal Rooster is analytical and hard-working. Compromise may be difficult for them, and they may feel unappreciated at times. In actuality nothing could be further from the truth, as Metal Roosters are indispensable to their family, friends, and employers. Metal Roosters are the most opinionated and verbal of all the Roosters. Powerfully candid, the Metal Rooster has a gift for captivating an audience with his shrewd and brilliant powers of deduction.

The Metal Dog is not as influenced by external circumstances as the other Dog Element combinations; determined and extremely success-oriented, this independent thinker follows her own path. If there is a flaw in someone or something, the Metal Dog will spot it. These Dogs are not as encumbered by the usual Dog anxiety, but their principles of loyalty and honesty remain quite rigid. The Metal Dog will vacillate between a desire for material success and an equally strong desire for spiritual reflection. They are more serious than other Dogs and remain idealistic realists.

The Metal Pig likes the definite and the predictable in life, and will tend to scrutinize everything with his most analytical eye. The most rigid of the Pig Element combinations, the Metal Pig can, at times, throw away a good situation because it does not conform to expectations. Metal Pigs enjoy success and are ambitious and clear sighted. They possess a warmer and more outgoing nature than other Pig Element combinations, and therefore usually enjoy a larger circle of friends.

Water

The Water Element expresses feelings, reflection, sensitivity, and persuasion. Symbolic of feelings and emotions, Water descends, seeks out, and fills low places—especially the hearts of the disheartened and needy. Those born into the Water Element are guided by their feelings and their need to communicate. The Water Element endows one with a lucid and quick mind; however, this Element is chaotic because it does not have its own form. Rather, it tends to take on the shape of whatever contains it.

Water Element lovers have the ability to persuade others and manipulate their environment. The Water Element also brings the gift of empathy and bestows a calmer and more sedate nature to each sign. Water Element natives view life subjectively, but their empathic and calming presence makes them much sought after for their counsel. The Water Element blesses its natives with a deep spiritual nature and ability to thrive in many social contexts. Those born into Water years possess extraordinary intuition and function as a kind of spiritual barometer in this life.

If you born under the Water Element:

* Your sexual style is submissive, masochistic, and mystical.
* Your predominant sense is hearing.
* You assist/help partners born into Wood years.
* You are assisted by partners born into Metal years.
* Your dominant traits are emotionality, clairvoyance, wisdom, and communication, but also excessive emotion and fear.

If you are yang Water "Ren" (Water Rat, Water Tiger, Water Dragon, Water Horse, Water Monkey, or Water Dog):

* Sudden wealth—yang Fire Bing
* Entitled wealth—yin Fire Ding
* Resources/contentment—yin Metal Xin

* Controller/positive change—yin Earth Ji
* Controller/unfavorable conflict—yang Earth Wu

If you are yin Water "Gui" (Water Ox, Water Rabbit, Water Snake, Water Goat, Water Rooster, or Water Pig):

* Sudden wealth—yin Fire Ding
* Entitled wealth—yang Fire Bing
* Resources/contentment—yang Metal Geng
* Controller/positive change—yang Earth Wu
* Controller/unfavorable conflict—yin Earth Ji

Water Element Combinations

The Water Rat is an open-minded Rat, always looking for new ideas and experiences. This is a very sensitive soul who empathizes with others. With their fine vocabulary and vivid imagination, Water Rats excel in language, writing, and journalism. This Rat knows how to communicate, and could easily influence the populace. The Water Element produces a soul who is deeply emotional and more introverted than other Rats.

The Water Ox has a knack for accurately predicting future trends and utilizing the talents and resources of others. The Water Ox will be able to wear away at even the toughest "rock" in life with his silent yet constant efforts. This intuitive Ox prefers to infiltrate rather than dominate, as other Ox Element combinations do. Water Oxen have a way with words and a talent that causes others to want what they want, thus achieving their goals in an indirect way.

The Water Tiger is an empathetic, humanitarian soul, and has a more serene and sedate nature than other Tigers. These are the dreamers and the artists of the Tiger kingdom. Their manner is less brusque and their edges are not as rough as their Tiger counterparts. They are blessed with judicious insight—many with a "sixth sense"—into human nature. The Water Tiger is exquisitely sensitive, and many pursue positions of spiritual leadership.

The Water Rabbit is sensitive and well-liked. The Water Element highlights and intensifies the already sensitive nature of the Rabbit sign. This Rabbit's thin-skinned and easily hurt feelings can be soothed with plenty of tender loving care and liberal doses of the finer things in life. The Water Rabbit is a deep thinker and possesses enhanced intuition bordering on the psychic. They are admired for their good taste and are highly valued for their advice.

The Water Dragon is extremely gifted and has a calmer and more sedate nature than other Dragon Element combinations. This is a liberal-minded Dragon, always open to new ideas and experiences. They have a true gift for seeing things objectively and for creating a solid foundation in all that they do. The humane Water Dragon is an excellent judge of the truth, and excels in any type of public relations work or public speaking.

The Water Snake is charismatic, compassionate, and capable. With their insightful and intuitive radar, they have a well-developed ability for communicating with others. They are "empaths" with a multitude of interests. Although they are born under the emotional and subjective Water Element, Water Snakes have a gift for seeing things objectively—their peculiar combination of sign and Element creates a compassionate and astute judge of human character. Because of this, Water Snakes are often highly sought after as advisors and financiers.

The Water Horse advances her ideas through her convincing speech, thereby influencing the thoughts of others. This is an open-minded Horse, always seeking new ideas and experiences. They have a gift for seeing things objectively and are viewed as humorous and friendly. The Water Horse is able to convey her emotions powerfully, and has an insatiable need for movement and decisive action.

The Water Goat is the most sensual of the Goat family. Although they possess remarkable street smarts, they require a great deal of emotional support. Loyalty is of supreme importance to the Water Goat. Amongst the Water Goats you can find many talented writers, poets, artists, and performers. The Water Goat is the most peace-loving and determinedly humanitarian of all the Goats.

The Water Monkey is tolerant and thoughtful. More inclined to moderation than other Monkey element combinations, they rarely take themselves too seriously and are full of humor and good cheer. The Water Monkey has a deep need to communicate with others. They cannot tolerate boredom, routine, or stagnation of their keen mind. Water Monkeys possess a stealthy nature, and further their cause indirectly by influencing and persuading others.

The Water Rooster is energetic and possesses an enjoyable sense of humor. They do, however, have a tendency to worry excessively at times. This is the intellectual type of Rooster who will enjoy cultural pursuits. With Water as this Rooster's Element, they will be given to clear thinking and compassion. The Water Rooster is proficient in the use of the written word, and is a commanding speaker with the ability to sway others' opinions.

The Water Dog is talented and intuitive. Others see them as kind and compassionate, and they can be very persuasive for the right cause. The Water Element makes the already tenderhearted Dog exceptionally empathetic and capable of great sacrifice. Always scrupulous and virtuous, the Water Dog's principal quality is loyalty. Occasionally lacking self-confidence, this emotional Dog needs much encouragement from others to assuage his self-doubt.

The Water Pig is shy and quiet, yet able to express herself articulately. They are hardworking and loyal, but may have felt restrained during the early periods in life. Competition does not interest them in the least—what they seek is peace and tranquility. The most private of the Pig family, the Water Pig is intuitive to the point of clairvoyance. They prefer to live within a safe and comfortable world of love and affection.

Note: If you are familiar with the "Four Pillars" Ba Zi sub-specialty of Chinese Astrology, and you know your "day master" Element (the Element ruling the day you were born), this can provide additional insight into your Elemental compatibility. This knowledge can also be used to see how you will fare in various years.

ELEMENTS

	Wood	Fire	Earth	Metal	Water
Color	Green	Red	Yellow/Brown	White	Black/Blue
Season	Spring	Summer	Between Season	Fall	Winter
Direction	East	South	Center	West	North
Food	Sour	Bitter	Sweet	Spicy	Salty
Fruit	Palm	Almond	Date	Peach	Chestnut
Organ	Liver	Heart	Spleen	Lungs	Kidneys
System	Nervous	Circulatory	Digestive	Respiratory	Excretory
Face	Eyes	Tongue	Mouth	Nose	Ears
Emotion	Anger	Happy	Worry	Sad	Fear
Weather	Windy	Hot	Wet	Dry	Cold
Personal	Honest	Polite	Loyal	Famous	Gentle

PART 11

MIND CONNECTIONS

Where the mind moves, the qi gathers.

—Chinese Taoist

CHAPTER 10

鼠牛虎兔龍蛇馬羊猴鶏犬猪

READYING THE MIND FOR EXTRAORDINARY SEX

SEX DRIVE CAN VARY GREATLY FROM ONE TIME to another, and can change depending on where our minds are and where our thoughts are focused. In fact, our sexual desire begins long before we reach the bedroom. According to the Tao, we are energized by beauty—by bringing beauty and those things that please the senses into our lives, we expand our desire. Readying the mind for sex is all about directing and focusing our energies. So before coming together with your lover, spend some time alone thinking about the things you love the most about him or her. Imagine his or her physique or wonderful scent, or envision that certain smile that turns you on so much.

Western views of the mind were reborn in 1929. It was then that renowned psychologist Carl G. Jung met a man named Richard Wilhelm, whose ideas were to change the course of the Western understanding of human behavior and bridge the philosophical gap that existed between East and West. In fact, Jung's "confrontation with the unconscious" was merely a rewriting of his newfound understanding of Chinese wisdom after studying the *I Ching* and Taoist alchemy. This wisdom teaches that mental control and enlightenment can be achieved through techniques such as controlled breathing, meditation, and special sexual practices. Taoist sexuality stresses the importance of the frame of mind when engaging in physical love. Psychological and spiritual forces are stored as memories in the body and are the basic material for harmonizing the physical with the mental.

In the past few decades, the realization of the unity of spirit, mind, and body (a paradigm disseminated in the West largely thanks to Jung) finds many in the East and West following similar paths. For many, self-esteem and self-concept are critical components in forming one's mental attitude and thinking about relationships and sexuality. In contrast to the Judeo-Christian doctrine that teaches the heart of a man is "desperately wicked and deceitful," the Eastern Taoist conception of humanity stringently protests this mentality, teaching instead that our bodies are "the very residence of our Creator," a testament to his existence and to the essence of love itself. The "end times" philosophy of some modern evangelical movements—with the hyperbole of the coming destruction of humanity—is also quite the mental bummer. The whole "desperately wicked" way of thinking, combined with possibility of armageddon by noon tomorrow, is pretty depressing and not very conducive to an attitude of joy, mindfulness, or healthy self-esteem. In contrast, Taoist sexuality enjoins the embracing of, and delight in, all of the pleasures that this life has to offer. This is not a philosophy of self-denial, self-loathing, and suffering, but rather one of self-elevation, enjoyment, and appreciation.

There is a universal parable, told in different ways within different cultures, that illustrates the power of the conscious mind. Here is the Chinese version of it:

An old Master was teaching his students about life. He said to them, "A battle is raging inside me—it is a terrible fight between two Tigers. One Tiger represents fear, anger, envy, selfishness, regret, arrogance, self-pity, shame, resentment, false pride, superiority, and ego. The other Tiger represents joy, peace, graciousness, humility, kindness, forgiveness, friendship, empathy, generosity, compassion, and faith."

He continued, "The same fight is going on inside each one of you."

The students thought about this for a while, until one of the students asked his Master, "Which Tiger will win?"

The old Master replied, "The one you feed."

CHAPTER 11

鼠牛虎兔龍蛇馬羊猴鷄犬豬

RESOLVING BLOCKS
TO INTIMACY

HAPPINESS AND MISFORTUNE ALWAYS WALK the same street. I am no stranger to love's bliss or its pain. I share with my human brothers and sisters a lifelong search for that enigmatic state called "true love." While the concept of looking at the glass of love as half-full rather than half-empty is a simple one, it is far from an easy thing to do. Most of us start out on life's path idealistic and hopeful, only to be disillusioned as we discover the cruel and insensitive side of love. Many have searched for love in all the wrong places, giving their power to another to make or break their happiness, and known the agony of unrequited love. At times, you yourself may have felt that love was not in the stars for you. I have personally made some less than ideal (okay, terrible) decisions, and then lamented the result. I have also made some equally good choices, the result of which brought me happiness, contentment, and peace of mind.

I am competent to council on just about every romantic blunder that a human can make and I have come to the conclusion that the root of romantic unhappiness is a dissatisfied mind. I say dissatisfied because we are often trying to force a "square peg into a round hole," romantically speaking. Unrealistic expectations are the mother of all disappointments!

Making good love choices requires knowledge of ourselves, knowledge of others, and the courage to believe that romantic happiness will be offered at the right time and with the right person.

Soul mates will share a life goal and work together to achieve it. They are spiritually and mentally on the same page. Under less ideal circumstances, one's potential, joy, and higher purpose can all be destroyed by uniting with the wrong individual. True soul mates support each other, forgive past mistakes, and allow human fragility in the relationship. For the brokenhearted, the disappointed, and the embittered, there is no more healing energy than making good love choices!

Each moment of each day we choose whether to view ourselves as victims or victors, blessed or blasted. Entering a union with our eyes wide open greatly determines our romantic fate. By using the three-part system in this book, you will be able to greatly increase your chances for finding, nurturing, and sustaining the relationship of your dreams.

Obstructions to Connection

In the quest for romantic happiness, it is crucial that we free ourselves of resentments from past disappointments. Tumultuous relationships are usually chock full of past karma. Consuming, passionate, and occasionally obsessive, these pairings are intense and instantaneous. To purposefully choose a rendezvous such as this takes courage, and is the astral signature of an evolved spirit. So what happens when one person is ready to confront and work out past issues but the other is not? When presented with the option, the reluctant party may jump ship. When this happens, the excruciating sting of rejection strikes at the very core of one's soul. While one of these "doozies" can age you 10 years or more, they do develop character and are a catalyst for growth. Bitterness is a toxic companion that will consume from the inside out, so we must realize that all passing "flames in the wind" are, in the long run, necessary and helpful. They serve to make us who we are today.

We never stop loving those whom we have truly loved. Every past attachment serves as part of a greater purpose or a bigger picture. You would not be who and where you are in this life if you were still with them; and you could not be who and where you are today if they had never crossed your path. This attitude of relativity seems simple enough, but the inability to forgive is at the core of what prevents many from being receptive to a soul mate.

Also, remember that you have to intensely love another person in order to intensely hate them. John Milton's famous quote, "torment, and loud lament, and furious rage," puts it well. Quiet contentment is the holy grail of the obsessive love crowd, and is a signpost of healing when it is attained. Relationships generally end when the lessons particular to that interaction are learned. However, if your spiritual connection with someone is strong because of a lot of past history, and the relationship is severed, the loss can feel unbearable. This can be seen most acutely with the soul mate connections. Some examples:

* If a Rat and an Ox team up and then part ways, either or both may hold on to the relationship with a death grip.

* If the Tiger and the Pig combine their energies and are abruptly split, either or both may be forever devastated.

* A Rabbit and a Dog are a volatile soul mate brew—if the detached Rabbit calls it quits, the attached Dog could self-destruct (and vice versa).

* A Dragon and a Rooster splitting up can make the Fourth of July seem quiet. Both are capable of making a memorable scene.

* The Snake and the Monkey who part ways or have a third party come between them can give new meaning to the words jealousy and scheming.

The disillusioned romantic mind is akin to a muddy glass of water; our disappointments are the impurities (the mud) that can be removed to reveal our true, pure love nature. Happiness is our birthright, but it is also a conscious choice. By freeing our minds of past bitterness, disappointments, and dissatisfactions, we become spiritually open and ready to love. Put more positively, we eliminate the blocks to intimacy and emotional afflictions by consciously and deliberately cultivating compassion, love, tolerance, and forgiveness.

Joy is in everything. One has only to extract it.

—Confucius

There are other, more prosaic blocks to intimacy. Stress, physical illness (a good physical check-up can be very helpful in diagnosing any metabolic lack of desire), hormonal changes, and certain medications (antidepressants, birth-control pills, and blood pressure medications are infamous) are the biggest culprits.

Barring the need for hormone replacement or other medically recommended treatments, Traditional Chinese Medicine (TCM) recommends adding the following foods to your diet in order to ignite libido and increase sexual desire:

* Shrimp
* Chinese chive
* Lamb
* Beef
* Walnuts
* Carrots
* Rice
* Royal jelly (honey)
* Gou qi zi (lycium fruit)

Of these foods, lycium fruit is the most potent, and is the most highly recommended by traditionalists. More exotic aphrodisiacs available from a Chinese herbalist include turtle, gecko, and deer horn (see more about foods and sexual supplements in Chapter 13).

The Dark Side of Love

Barring past relationship stings, bitterness, or physical illness, there is another realm to explore that can be the culprit for blocking intimacy—the full-fledged personality disorder. Estimates say that anywhere from 1 to 3 percent of the population suffers from a major personality disorder. As our personality consists of a predisposed "temperament" (astrological influence) and a learned disposition of "character" (present consciousness), a personality disorder develops as a learned coping mechanism when something goes terribly wrong with our earthly environment in early development. Thought to be caused by trauma in infancy or childhood, most major personality disorders gain strength in adolescence and early adulthood, when they begin to seriously interfere with the individual's spiritual, mental, and physical relationships.

The *Diagnostic and Statistical Manual of Mental Disorders* (DSM-IV-TR), published by the American Psychiatric Association, currently defines a personality disorder as an enduring pattern of inner experience and behavior that deviates markedly from the expectation of the individual's culture, is pervasive, inflexible, and leads to distress or impairment.

These pervasive and chronic psychological disorders of "self" can run the gamut from mild to severe, and can greatly affect a person's life and derail the course of love. While most normal people have some neuroses and odd quirks, the person with a full-fledged personality disorder can resemble a boat in a hurricane.

In such disorders, the true self (xian tian) is almost completely absent, becoming replaced instead by a "false self." This is a case of the spirit and personality being completely incommunicado. People with personality disorders share several distinct features including (but not limited to): a disturbed self-image, the inability to have successful romantic relationships, a lack of boundaries, and bizarre ways of thinking and perceiving others.

When involved in a dysfunctional love/sexual relationship with a personality-disordered individual, you often know something is wrong but you can't quite put your finger on it. These disturbances are not just occasional (for example, surfacing only under stress); rather, they represent a pervasive pattern of behavior that departs radically from what society considers normal. As a result, people with such disorders often experience chronic conflicts with others.

There are 10 different types of major personality disorders, each with a different underlying theme. (But be forewarned—these disorders tend to cluster together in groups of twos and threes.) For instance, people suffering from a narcissistic personality disorder respond with extreme defensiveness when they feel that their self-perception (as someone special and privileged) has been threatened. Similarly, those suffering with borderline personality disorder respond extremely negatively to perceived abandonment, and those with antisocial personality disorder lack normal feelings of responsibility and compassion and thus have little motivation to restrain their reactions.

The specifics differ but all personality disorders have certain things in common:

* Self-centeredness (me, me, me).

* Victim mentality (blaming others, society, and/or the universe for their problems).

* Lack of accountability (rules don't apply to them).

* Lack of perspective and ability to empathize.

* Exploitive or manipulative behavior.

* Unhappiness, depression, and/or anxiety disorders.

* Distorted view of self and others.
* Inability to see behavior as unacceptable or acknowledge destructive behaviors.

Having one or two of these characteristics doesn't necessarily make a person personality disordered; however, five or more may be a sign of something to be concerned about. If you are involved with someone you recognize here, please RUN, don't walk to the nearest exit. You cannot "fix" them (although some signs such as the Dog and the Pig often try), and most who attempt to end up forming support groups or making a psychiatrist rich.

Antisocial Personality Disorder

Someone with this disorder exhibits a long-standing pattern of a disregard for other people's rights, often crossing the line, acting out, and violating those rights. These people are identified by a lack of regard for the moral or legal standards in the local culture, as well as a marked inability to get along with others or abide by societal rules. They are sometimes called psychopaths or sociopaths.

Character traits:

* Clashes frequently with law enforcement.
* Is deceitful—lies, uses aliases, or cons others for personal profit or pleasure.
* Is impulsive—fails to anticipate consequences.
* Is irritable and aggressive—engages in frequent physical fights or assaults.
* Disregards the safety of self or others.
* Exhibits long-term irresponsibility—failure to stay employed, work behavior problems.
* Demonstrates a lack of remorse for, indifference toward, or the rationalizing of having hurt, mistreated, or stolen from another.

Avoidant Personality Disorder

This disorder is characterized by a long-standing and complex pattern of feelings of inadequacy, extreme sensitivity to criticism, and marked social inhibition.

Character traits:

* Avoids careers or social activities that involve significant interpersonal contact because of fears of criticism, disapproval, or rejection.
* Is unwilling to get involved with people unless certain of being liked.
* Is resistant to intimacy because of the fear of being shamed or ridiculed.
* Is preoccupied with being criticized or rejected in social situations.
* Is inhibited in new interpersonal situations because of feelings of inadequacy.
* Views self as inferior or personally unappealing to others.
* Is reluctant to take personal risks or to engage in any new activities because they may prove embarrassing.

Borderline Personality Disorder

This disorder is characterized by a history of changeable and unstable personal relationships, as well as rapidly fluctuating affections or feelings. Relationships can be fickle and shallow. This person may exhibit impulsive behaviors, lack of identity, and rapid mood changes.

Character traits:

* Makes dramatic efforts to avoid real or imagined abandonment.
* Maintains unstable and intense interpersonal relationships alternating between extremes of idealization and devaluation.
* Exhibits identity disturbance—a markedly and persistently unstable self-image or sense of self.
* Shows impulsivity in at least two areas that are potentially self-damaging (spending, sex, substance abuse, gambling, reckless driving, binge eating).
* Engages in suicidal behavior, gestures, or threats, or self-mutilating behavior.
* Experiences intense episodic depression, irritability, or anxiety usually lasting a few hours and only rarely more than a few days.

* Experiences chronic feelings of emptiness.
* Demonstrates inappropriate, intense anger or difficulty controlling anger.

Dependent Personality Disorder

People suffering from this disorder exhibit a need to be taken care of and a fear of being abandoned or separated from important individuals. This pervasive fear of abandonment leads to excessive "clinging," submissive behavior, an extreme need of other people, and the inability to be independent. These people also exhibit a marked lack of decisiveness and self-confidence.

Character traits:

* Has difficulty making everyday decisions without advice and reassurance from others.
* Needs others to assume responsibility for major areas of his or her life.
* Has difficulty expressing disagreement with others because of fear of loss of support or approval.
* Has difficulty initiating projects or doing things on his or her own because of a lack of self-confidence in judgment or abilities, rather than a lack of motivation or energy.
* Goes to excessive lengths to obtain care and support from others, to the point of volunteering for unpleasant tasks.
* Is uncomfortable when alone because of exaggerated fears of being unable to care for him- or herself.
* When a relationship ends, he or she urgently seeks another relationship as a source of care and support.

Histrionic Personality Disorder

Excessive emotionality and attention-seeking mark these individuals. They can exhibit exaggerated and often inappropriate displays of emotional reactions, often approaching the theatrical.

Character traits:

* Is uncomfortable in situations in which they are not the center of attention.

* Interacts with others in a way that is inappropriate or sexually seductive behavior.

* Displays rapidly shifting expression of emotions.

* Consistently uses physical appearance to draw attention to self.

* Has a style of speech that is dramatic, outdated, or metaphoric.

* Exhibits self-dramatization, theatricality, and exaggerated expression of emotion.

* Is suggestible and easily influenced by others or circumstances.

* Considers relationships to be more intimate than they actually are.

Narcissistic Personality Disorder

This person will exhibit grandiosity in fantasy or behavior, an excessive need for admiration, and a lack of empathy. They are unable to see the viewpoints of others, but are hypersensitive to the opinions of others.

Character traits:

* Has an exaggerated sense of self-importance.

* Expects special treatment without commensurate accomplishments.

* Exaggerates achievements and talents.

* Is preoccupied with fantasies of brilliant success, power, beauty, or ideal love.

* Believes that he or she is special and unique and can only be understood by, or should associate with, other special or high-status people or organizations.

* Requires excessive admiration.

* Has a sense of entitlement and unreasonably expects favorable treatment automatically.

* Is interpersonally exploitative and "uses" others to achieve his or her own ends.

* Lacks empathy—is unwilling to recognize or identify with the feelings and needs of others.

* Is often envious of others and/or believes that others are envious of him or her.

* Shows arrogant, haughty behaviors or attitudes.

Obsessive-Compulsive Personality Disorder

Not to be confused with Obsessive-Compulsive Disorder, this disorder of anxiety is characterized by a preoccupation with orderliness, perfectionism, and mental and interpersonal control. These individuals can be plagued by inflexibility and a preoccupation with uncontrollable thoughts and actions.

Character traits:

* Is preoccupied with details, rules, lists, order, organization, or schedules to the extent that the major point of the activity is lost.

* Exhibits a perfectionism that interferes with completing projects—overly strict standards.

* Is a "workaholic," or excessively devoted to work and productivity.

* Is overconscientious, scrupulous, and inflexible about matters of morality, ethics, or values (excepting those grounded in cultural or religious beliefs).

* Is unable to discard worn-out or worthless objects, even when they have no sentimental value.

* Is reluctant to delegate tasks or to work with others unless they submit to exactly his or her way of doing things.

* Adopts a miserly spending style toward both self and others; money is viewed as something to be hoarded for future catastrophes.

* Shows rigidity and stubbornness—lacks flexibility.

Paranoid Personality Disorder

People with this disorder show an extreme distrust and suspiciousness of others; all motives are interpreted as malicious. They hold a belief, without reason, that others are exploiting, harming, betraying, or trying to deceive them. They find hidden meanings everywhere and in everything. They also tend to be unforgiving and grudge-holding.

Character traits:

* Suspects, without sufficient basis, that others are exploiting, harming, or deceiving him or her.
* Is preoccupied with doubts about the loyalty or trustworthiness of friends and family.
* Is reluctant to confide in others because of unwarranted fear that the information will be used against him or her.
* Sees hidden demeaning or threatening intent behind innocent remarks or events.
* Persistently bears grudges, and is unforgiving of insults, injuries, or slights (real or imagined).
* Perceives attacks on character or reputation that are not apparent to others.
* Is quick to react angrily or to counterattack.
* Has recurrent suspicions, without justification, regarding the fidelity of a spouse or sexual partner.

Schizoid Personality Disorder

This disorder is characterized by a detachment from social relationships and limited range of expression and experiencing of emotions. These people seem indifferent to social relationships.

Character traits:

* Does not desire or enjoy very close relationships, including being part of a family.
* Almost always chooses solitary activities.
* Has little, if any, interest in sex.
* Takes pleasure in few, if any, activities.
* Lacks close friends or confidants other than first-degree relatives.
* Appears indifferent to the praise or criticism of others.
* Appears emotionally cold, detached, or dejected.

Schizotypal Personality Disorder

Someone with this disorder exhibits an extreme discomfort with, and reduced capacity for, close relationships. They demonstrate perceptual distortions and eccentricities of behavior, including peculiarities of thinking; eccentricities of appearance, behavior, and interpersonal style; and magical thinking.

Character traits:

* Maintains odd beliefs or bizarre fantasies that dominate behavior (such as thinking one is Christ, Buddha, an alien from another solar system, and so on).

* Experiences visual hallucinations.

* Thinks or speaks in a way that is vague, dramatic, or metaphorical.

* Demonstrates suspiciousness or paranoid ideation.

* Behaves or appears in a way that is odd, eccentric, and/or peculiar, or that significantly violates social customs.

* Lacks close friends or confidants other than first-degree relatives.

* Has excessive social anxiety that does not diminish with familiarity and tends to be associated with paranoid fears rather than negative judgments about self.

The Disturbed Rat

In contrast to their healthy counterparts, personality-disordered Rats can be covert and secretive, and will deflect or mislead if it is to their advantage. They can be difficult to please, demanding, and highly critical of others. Often their standards are unreasonable, and impossible for their partner to uphold. Despite surface composure, Rats may also be gnawed by a devastating feeling of insecurity that causes them to act out. A disturbed Rat will gladly take full advantage of those around them. Profiteering and opportunistic behavior represents their energy being directed in its most unproductive form; expressed in its darkest form, this energy becomes: dishonesty, agitation, restlessness, neurosis, aggressiveness, pettiness, hypochondria, and materialism. Taken to an extreme, histrionic, borderline, or avoidant personality disorders may develop.

The Disturbed Ox

In contrast to their healthy counterparts, personality disordered Oxen can be overly stern and even volatile, and be so rigid as to become immovable, even when the situation requires otherwise. An Ox hates being contradicted, especially in front of others, and can be subject to explosive outbreaks of anger. Oxen do not enjoy being teased, and possess a choleric temperament. They also dislike insubordination, defiance, and disloyalty of any kind. Disturbed Oxen are capable of holding grudges for long durations and are known for serving their revenge cold. Authoritarianism and extreme rigidity represent the Ox's energy being directed in its most unproductive form; expressed in its darkest form, this energy becomes: possessiveness, brooding, stubbornness, lack of empathy, cruelty, jealousy, spite, malice, and revenge. Taken to an extreme, antisocial, schizoid, or narcissistic personality disorders can develop.

The Disturbed Tiger

In contrast to their healthy counterparts, personality-disordered Tigers can be careless, obstinate, and rebellious. If their pride is involved, they will cut off their nose to spite their face. Recklessness, oppositional defiance, and hasty action without forethought represents the Tiger's energy being directed in its most unproductive form; expressed in it's darkest form, this energy becomes: rebellion to the point of foolishness, toughness, envy, carelessness, bossiness, and imprudent thrill-seeking to the point of injuring themselves or others. Impulse-control problems and rebellion against any kind of perceived authority is a common theme amongst disturbed Tigers. Taken to an extreme, their sense of "empowered entitlement" can become a full-fledged case of narcissistic or antisocial personality disorder.

The Disturbed Rabbit

In contrast to their healthy counterparts, personality-disordered Rabbits can be aloof, secretive, and petty. Rabbits run away when being forced to choose sides or make difficult choices anyway, and a disturbed Rabbit will give new meaning to the words "commitment phobic." As one of the most sexual of signs, disordered Rabbits relish the role of the Don Juan or femme fatale, leaving a trail of broken hearts and shirked responsibilities in their wake. Rabbits in general hate to take the blame for anything, but personality-disordered Rabbits truly excel at "passing the buck." Self-centered, shallow, and brittle behavior represents the Rabbit's energy being directed in its most unproductive form; expressed in its darkest form, this energy becomes: disloyalty, cowardice, selfishness, narcissism, self-absorption, materialism, arrogance, and exhibitionism. Taken to an extreme, narcissistic, histrionic, and borderline personality disorders can develop.

The Disturbed Dragon

In contrast to their healthy counterparts, personality-disordered Dragons can be short-tempered, demanding, and cruelly candid. Being a soul of extremes, the Dragon's energy channeled negatively can cause great destruction. Disturbed Dragons can blurt out whatever is on their minds, consequences be damned, and may act as though they rule by divine right. They are capable of maintaining a completely separate life from their partner, sometimes for years. Not surprisingly, infidelity is one of their most unattractive traits. Egotistic and judgmental behavior represents the Dragon's energy being directed in its most unproductive form; expressed in its darkest form, this energy becomes: easy infatuation, verbal brutality, manic-depression, belligerence, problem-making, mean-spirited or cruel behavior, and anarchy. Taken to an extreme, schizotypal, narcissistic, and antisocial personality disorders are seen.

The Disturbed Snake

In contrast to their healthy counterparts, personality-disordered Snakes can be covert and secretive, and may vacillate between being extravagant and stingy. They guard their possessions—objects or people—doggedly. Disturbed Snakes have been known to be shameless philanderers and hedonists. Laziness and procrastination are some of the Snake's most irritating personality quirks. Jealous and possessive behavior represents the Snake's energy being directed in its most unproductive form; expressed in it's darkest form, this energy becomes: dishonesty, procrastination, stubbornness, vengefulness, lethargy, and odd, eccentric, or peculiar behavior. Taken to an extreme, schizotypal, avoidant, and paranoid personality disorders are seen.

The Disturbed Horse

In contrast to their healthy counterparts, personality-disordered Horses can be infatuate, hotheaded, and incredibly selfish. The shadow side of the Horse is far from their cheerful and self-assured lighter side. Dysfunctional Horses believe that this world and everything in it revolves around them. Their house, their car, their school, their life—it's all about them. Tactless and ruthless behavior represents the Horse's energy being directed in its most unproductive form; expressed in its darkest form, this energy becomes: egomaniacal behavior, aggression, zealotry, rashness, and fanaticism. Taken to an extreme, narcissistic, obsessive-compulsive, and antisocial disorders occur.

The Disturbed Goat

In contrast to their healthy counterparts, personality-disordered Goats can be irresponsible, undisciplined, and unreliable. An obsessive-compulsive Goat with impulse-control issues can easily squander a small fortune or run up astronomical expenses. Dysfunctional Goats are dissatisfied malcontents who depend too heavily on others. Although they prefer to be followers, they will not hesitate to complain bitterly when things don't go their way. Self-indulgent and irresponsible behavior represents the Goat's energy being directed in its most unproductive form; expressed in its darkest form, this energy becomes: extreme laziness, procrastination, dependence, pessimism, perpetual tardiness, prudishness, and a victim mentality. Taken to an extreme, obsessive-compulsive, schizotypal, and avoidant personality disorders are found.

The Disturbed Monkey

In contrast to their healthy counterparts, personality-disordered Monkeys are manipulative, opportunistic, and status seeking. A disturbed Monkey hides a low opinion and secret distrust of other people behind an outward friendliness. Suspicious and snobbish behavior represents the Monkey's energy being directed in its most unproductive form. When the Monkey's complicated and dubious personality becomes skewed, the following interpersonal problems can result: trickery, infidelity, vanity, distrust, self-interest, perversion, and juvenile behavior. Taken to an extreme, paranoid, antisocial, and borderline personality disorders are seen.

The Disturbed Rooster

In contrast to their healthy counterparts, personality-disordered Roosters can be vain, hairsplitting, and downright cruel. The shadow side of the Rooster reveals sadism, vanity, and an obsession with appearance. Perfectionistic and highly critical of others, they hurl caustic comments at will. Well-balanced Roosters are enchanting, but disturbed Roosters are absolutely unbearable. Sarcastic and harsh behavior represents the Rooster's energy being directed in its most unproductive form; expressed in its darkest form, this energy becomes: causticity, pomposity, tactlessness, mean-spiritedness, sadism, and braggadocio. Taken to an extreme, sadistic, narcissistic, and antisocial behavior develops.

The Disturbed Dog

In contrast to their healthy counterparts, personality-disordered Dogs are agitated, secretive, and paranoid. Condescending and moralizing, emotionally disturbed Dogs are personifications of the "prophet of doom." They are also prone to obsessive, dysfunctional relationships with troubled partners. Masochism, acid words, and paranoid behavior represents the Dog's energy being directed in its most unproductive form; expressed in its darkest form, this energy becomes: panic attacks, anxiety, agitation, pessimism, introversion, paranoia, cryptic speech, fanaticism, and major depression. Taken to an extreme, dependent, schizoid, and obsessive-compulsive personality disorders may develop.

The Disturbed Pig

In contrast to their healthy counterparts, personality-disordered Pigs can be passive, self-indulgent, and apathetic. The Pig's passive-aggressive personality allows them to avoid having to make decisions. The Pig's search for earthly pleasures can blind them, and lead them down a carnal path of fetishes and perversions of all types. Dysfunctional Pigs may deliberately choose difficult or neurotic partners. Expressed in its darkest form, the Pig's energy becomes: gullibility, defenselessness, penny-pinching, apathy, hypersensitivity, vengefulness, and reliance on physical and material comforts. Taken to an extreme, obsessive-compulsive, schizotypal, and avoidant personality disorders are found.

CHAPTER 12

鼠牛虎兔龍蛇馬羊猴鶏犬猪

THE SUPERIOR LOVER

*Only through daily self-renewal of character can
one continue at the height of power.*

—I Ching

The superior lover:

* Is humble.
* Is willing to let others go ahead.
* Offers their partner attention, support, affection, and humor.
* Is courteous.
* Has good manners.
* Is good-natured.
* Is calm.
* Feels compassion for others.
* Chooses battles wisely and yields to win..
* Gives others credit.
* Speaks well of everyone.
* Is physically fit.
* Practices moderation.

* Can cheerfully do without.
* Is able to make decisions.
* Likes to teach others.
* Is tolerant of faults.
* Is gentle.
* Is true to beliefs.
* Has nothing to prove.
* Is content.
* Laughs easily.
* Can cry.
* Is dependable.
* Is aware of danger.
* Has no hidden agendas.
* Honors others and is honored in kind.
* Pays attention to detail.
* Puts effort into staying connected.
* Is optimistic.
* Is considerate.
* Is fair.
* Causes others to feel special.
* Is forgiving.
* Holds no bitterness.
* Obtains nothing by force.
* Overlooks the mistakes of others.
* Leaves things better than the way they found them.
* Seeks enlightenment.
* Does not boast.
* Has endurance.
* Lives a simple life.
* Exists in the present.
* Nurtures good qualities.
* Depends on self for happiness.

CHAPTER 13

鼠牛虎兔龍蛇馬羊猴鶏犬猪

SEDUCTION AND ROMANCE, ATMOSPHERE AND AMBIANCE: SETTING THE MOOD

AN IDEAL WAY TO SET THE STAGE FOR satisfying seduction and remarkable romance is to nurture the senses with tantalizing scents, soothing ambiance, and relaxing music. Harmonize your love nest with subtle lighting, beautiful objects, and erotic scents to stimulate your romantic mind.

Erotic sights, smells, and sounds *increase* brain function in the hypothalamus and the occipital and frontal brain lobes. These same unconscious reactions from the senses simultaneously *decrease* activity in both of the brain's temporal lobes, which in turn deactivates inhibition, embarrassment, and moral judgment during sexual arousal. In contrast, when we are stressed, frightened, or angry, the adrenaline "fight or flight" hormones that block activation of the arousal areas of the brain and activate the temporal lobe (apprehension) areas are released. This causes inhibition and a lack of sexual desire. Stress, fear, anger, and adrenaline are the deathblows to a good sexual experience. The path to mind-blowing sex is paved with relaxation.

Aromatherapy for Lovers

There is a long and rich history of using the olfactory senses to enhance sexuality. The use of essential oils and scents for their aphrodisiacal effects stimulates the brain's limbic system to relax, to transform spiritually, and to come alive sexually. Some of these essential and precious oils come from herbs, roots, and bark, while others are derived from fruits, flowers, and seeds. For centuries they have been used for their meditative, calming, and beneficial properties. These essential oils can be released using an aroma lamp, by adding them to a warm bath, or by mixing them with a "carrier oil" for sensual massage.

A carrier oil is used as a base in massage oils and acts as a conduit that brings essential oils and other ingredients into the skin. Almond, grape seed, or jojoba oils are penetrating, light, and fast-absorbing, making them ideal for diluting these powerful essences. Avoid mineral or baby oil, as they tend to be too heavy. Use the recipes below or be creative and mix your own special potions. (Note: Never use pure essential oils directly on the skin without diluting them in a carrier oil. And, of course, always spot test first to make sure you or your partner isn't allergic!)

The essential oils are separated into two main categories: the stimulating yang oils and the relaxing yin oils. The yang or Emperor oils promote authority, financial prosperity, fathering, self-mastery, and sexual virility. They are the scents of choice to stimulate sexual passion and are also the most arousing to the male brain. The yin or Empress oils promote romantic love, nurturing, mothering, tranquility, and feminine powers of intuition. They are the scents of choice to create harmony, relaxation, and receptivity (eliminating the "fight or flight" hormones which block sexual pleasure and orgasm).

The yang or Emperor oils include:

* Black pepper—sharp, spicy, virility-enhancing
* Cedarwood—harmonious, meditative, woody
* Cinnamon—warm, spicy, sweet, aphrodisiacal
* Clary sage—warm, light, euphoric, protective
* Clove—pungent, sweet, spicy, warm
* Eucalyptus—bracing, mentally clarifying, medicinal
* Ginger—aromatic, aphrodisiacal, stimulating
* Musk, balsam—erotic, earthy
* Myrrh—balsamic, spicy, warming, calming
* Patchouli—smoky, earthy, erogenous
* Sandalwood—sweet, woody, erogenous
* Vanilla—warm, sweet, delicious, sensual

The yin or Empress oils include:

* Angelica root—aphrodisiacal
* Chamomile—pungent, herbal, calming, balancing
* Gardenia—sweet, euphoric, promotes feelings of well-being
* Geranium—light, flowery, promotes mental harmony
* Jasmine—honey-like, aphrodisiacal, anti-depressant
* Lavender—sweet, relaxing, cheering
* Lemon—fresh, light, mood-elevating
* Lotus blossom—delicate, enlightening, meditative
* Narcissus—sweet, erotic, floral
* Orange neroli—sweet/spicy orange blossom, promotes romantic love and tranquility
* Rose—sweet, promotes romantic love, dispels grief
* Rosemary—relaxing, stimulates sexual arousal
* Ylang-ylang—strong, sweet, erogenous

Water Play

A warm bath before making unforgettable love can increase the circulation in the sexual organs. Treat yourself and your lover to a bubble bath for two by candlelight. An aromatic bath of sandalwood, cypress, and vanilla (6–15 drops total per full bathtub) is a delicious prelude to lovemaking. For an extra-special treat, enrich the bath with honey or cream. In lieu of a bath, try putting a few drops of aromatic oil onto your shower head and enjoy!

Bath Oil Recipes

For stimulation, try these combinations:

* 5 drops patchouli, 2 drops sandalwood, 2 drops rose
* 4 drops musk, 3 drops balsam
* 5 drops sandalwood, 1 drop jasmine, 3 drops cedarwood
* 4 drops jasmine, 2 drops orange bergamot, 1 drop vanilla

For relaxation, try these combinations:

* 5 drops lavender, 3 drops ylang-ylang, 2 drops chamomile
* 5 drops lavender, 2 drops geranium

* 4 drops ylang-ylang, 2 drops orange neroli
* 5 drops vanilla, 2 drops angelica, 1 drop chamomile

If you desire to share a spiritually cleansing, traditional Taoist bath for two, fill your tub with warm water and stir in 1 cup of apple cider vinegar and 1 teaspoon of sea salt. Sink down into the soothing water and soak as you meditate, concentrating on removing any negative energy or stress you may feel. Wrap yourself in a soft cotton towel, air dry naturally, and continue to meditate for as long as you wish.

Colors and Candles

Colors act as a visual stimulus to our awareness. Our conscious and unconscious responses to colors run deep within the synapses of the brain. Colors are Elemental light radiations from the realm of the spirit. Each color of the rainbow allows us a sensory glimpse into the divine.

Candles not only contribute a pleasant ambiance to your cozy love lair, but they also stimulate the Fire Element responsible for feelings of passion, arousal, and resolution.

Each color of the quartz prism has its own unique erogenous qualities. Choose the mood and type of romance you wish to attract by selecting the corresponding candle color:

* Crimson/red—romance, strength, sexual passion
* Dark blue/indigo—alignment, bonding, soulmating with a partner
* Forest green—longevity, healing, fertility
* Gold—spiritual attainment
* Orange—increased energy and alertness
* Pink—gentleness, love, loyalty
* Purple/violet—spiritual awakening, enlightenment
* Sky/medium blue—safety, protection, relaxation
* White—new beginnings, purity, mercy
* Yellow—centering, communication

Sensual Massage

Sensual massage has long been used for health and happiness. It is a sure-fire way to get your lover into the romantic mood. However, specific massage techniques are not as important as you and your partner relaxing and enjoying each other. The most erotic "yin" body zones for women are the lips, tongue, nipples, and labia. The most erotic "yang" body zones for men are the earlobes, the nape of the neck, the top of the buttocks crack (where the sacrum and lumbar vertebrae meet), the inner thighs, and the top of the thighs on the outside where they meet the torso. In Taoist sexual ritual, these areas are kissed, nibbled, stroked, and caressed with essential oils until the partner is brought to ecstasy. Begin with the yang body zones and move gradually to the yin areas.

Aphrodisiacal Mixtures for Sensual Massage

Select your favorite essential oil and mix it together with 6 ounces of almond, grape seed, or jojoba oil to create an aromatic sensual massage oil. Use one of the classic combinations below, or create your own unique concoctions:

* 4 drops sandalwood, 2 drops jasmine, 1 drop rose
* 3 drops ylang-ylang, 3 drops sandalwood, 2 drops patchouli
* 4 drops lavender, 2 drops ylang-ylang, 2 drops chamomile

Music

As one of the great musical masters once said, "Music has the ability to pull the listener into the mind of the composer, helplessly and absolutely." For better or worse, our auditory senses are powerful and sensitive: While unwanted noise grates on the nerves and quickly becomes intolerable, enchanting and melodic melodies have the ability to create harmony and relaxation, and can positively transform our consciousness. Whether a classic such as Puccini's stirring aria from *Madame Butterfly*, Beethoven's "Moonlight Sonata," or an exquisite cello solo played by Yo-Yo Ma, use your favorite music to set just the right mood for you and your lover.

If your tastes run more to the modern classics, indulge in "Nights in White Satin" by the Moody Blues, the erotic beats of Enigma, or perhaps the sexy crooning of Chris Isaak in "Wicked Game." New Age lovers will enjoy musical artists such as Enya, Loreena McKennitt, and Deva Premal. Whether you choose the relaxing Chinese folk ballads of Cindy Mao, or the haunting Native American flute melodies of R. Carlos Nakai, great music has a peerless ability to set the mood for memorable lovemaking.

The Jade Bedchamber

Prepare your bedroom for passion using sensual textures and inviting fabrics such as silk, satin, velvet, and soft cottons. Rich colors of emerald green, indigo blue, and fuchsia can transform even the most boring bedroom into a sultry boudoir. Start with silk sheets in gold, top with an embroidered satin comforter in rich jewel tones, and accent with overstuffed velvet pillows. For a truly elegant look, make a simple canopy over your bed by draping your favorite material in one of several simple styles.

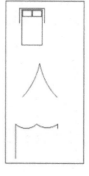

An innocent white cotton and lace motif is also very sexy, and a bed draped with a white gauze mosquito net makes for a romantic Casbah. Whatever style you choose, be sure to add some fresh flowers such as lilies, daisies, freesia, tulips, roses, gardenias, lilacs, or a romantic bouquet of wildflowers. Finally, tuck away some love snacks such as Godiva chocolates, fresh strawberries with whipped cream, or some chilled champagne if you would like. The only rules for entrance into your new love chamber are that you must leave your worldly stresses and worries at the door. Have fun!

Sexual Feng Shui

Feng shui is the ancient Chinese art of placement. Literally translated as "wind and water," feng shui utilizes the principles of the five Elements to choose harmonious shapes, colors, and directions in order to achieve balance and harmony. Ancient Taoists utilized feng shui not only for good business, luck, and fortune, but also for channeling the energy of relationships. This harmonizing of spirit and environment can be manipulated to create balance in our own love lives as well. By using some basic principles of feng shui we can create a unique and private retreat in which to reflect, to meditate, and to love.

Feng shui can put your love life on track by using the principles of wind and water. With these guidelines, you can create a balanced, relaxing, and harmonious environment conducive to love. Sexual potency flows generously in a bedroom that has a feeling of well-being, beauty, and comfort. Create your own ideal atmosphere using colors, textures, and the five essential Elements of Wood (houseplants, bonzai trees), Fire (candles, fireplaces, subdued lighting), Earth (flora, moss, soil), Metal (mirrors, chimes), and Water (indoor table-top fountains, aquariums, pictures of the ocean or waterfalls).

The northeast area of the bedroom is the "relationship" corner of the room and should be free of clutter. This is also where you should place your fragrant candles, flowers, a picture of your beloved, or even a cozy sitting area for two. Start your sexual energy flow with wavy or curved lines and shapes. Avoid sharp, straight, or pointed angular lines, which attract sha qi (negative sexual energy). Create a balance of yin (dark, soft, passive) and yang (light, hard, active) with plants, objects, and colors. Choose your overall feeling based on the balance of energy between you and your lover. For example, two overheated "yang" lovers may want to cool down with an understated, restrained, and subtle feeling in the bedroom, while two cool "yin" lovers may wish to stimulate their passion by choosing a bold, arousing, "dominant" look.

Keep in mind the productive/destructive and controlling/generating relationships between the five elements. For example, don't locate water, fountains, or aquariums in central (Earth Element) zones; fireplaces, candles, or heat sources in northern (Water Element) zones; plants and trees in western (Metal Element) areas; planting soil and flora in eastern (Wood Element) areas; or metal statues and chimes in southern (Fire Element) zones.

Here's how to apply basic feng shui principles in your home and bedroom: Determine the five directions and placements using a compass or a lo pan (a type of Chinese compass used exclusively in feng shui), or use the main entrance to your home as a reference point—known as the "eight point" method—to locate the various life areas.

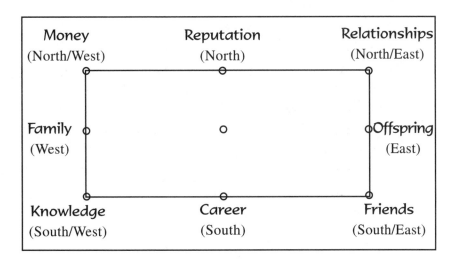

Then, superimpose the previous map over your individual bedroom or floor plan and decorate accordingly. Notice that the "relationship/marriage" area of your space is located in the northeast sector of the home and the northeast corner of the bedroom area.

1. North/Reputation/Black
   * Dreams
   * Aspirations
   * Awards
   * Fame
   * Achievement

2. Northwest/Money/Purple
   * Wealth
   * Abundance
   * Material possessions
   * Mentors and benefactors

3. West/Family/White
   * Rebirth and rejuvenation
   * Harmony
   * Health
   * Family life
   * Nutrition
   * Healing

4. Southwest/Knowledge/Pink
   * Wisdom
   * Spiritual and intellectual development
   * Meditation, reading, inner journeys

5. South/Career/Red
   * Opportunity
   * Happiness
   * Vitality
   * Energy
   * Trade
   * Interests outside of home

6. Southeast/Friends/Brown
   * Communication
   * Cultivating friendships
   * Socializing
   * Festivity
   * Helpful people
   * Supporters

7. East/Offspring/Green
   * Creativity
   * Personal growth
   * New ideas
   * Inspiration
   * New life and growth
   * Children

8. Northeast/Relationships/Blue
   * Marriage
   * Romance
   * Motherhood
   * Love
   * Relationships
   * Partners

In addition to these feng shui basics, the four peach blossom directions—north, south, east, and west—are stimulation locations for romantic love. By placing fresh flowers, fountains, or red or pink candles in these locations, new romance is said to be attracted. Your peach blossom sign/direction is calculated based on your Chinese animal sign:

* If you are a Rat, Dragon, or Monkey, your peach blossom is in the west under the sign of the Rooster.

* If you are an Ox, Snake, or Rooster, your peach blossom is in the south under the sign of the Horse.

* If you are a Tiger, Horse, or Dog, your peach blossom is in the east under the sign of the Rabbit.

* If you are a Rabbit, Goat, or Pig, your peach blossom is in the north under the sign of the Rat.

The Outdoors—Earthly Love

A garden is more than a place to connect with the earth: It can also be a place to connect with each other. On display at the Sexual Museum in Shanghai is an erotic plate from the 19th century showing a couple having sex in a garden. This was a reflection of the popular saying of the time: "Sex in the outdoors is worth a thousand experiences in a bed." Whether it's lying side-by-side on a balmy beach or a taking a moonlit walk through a snowy forest, sharing nature, fresh air, and physical exercise can be an invigorating prelude to making unforgettable love. Even the city has its own outdoor excitement with the bright glitz of lights, sights, and many other diversions. So find a secluded beach, a mountaintop at sunset, a cozy cabin in the woods, a bed and breakfast at a historic hotel, a boat cruise at sunset, or a cabin on your favorite lake. Other excellent possibilities are a full moon and a private beach, or a rendezvous on a hilltop for some exhilarating "night skiing" for two. Whatever your surroundings and individual style, sharing the outdoors with your lover makes for happy and healthy partners. T'ai chi and traditional qi gong are also wonderful for the reduction of stress and anxiety. As always, good health is a prerequisite for good sex!

Foods

From time immemorial, foods and herbs have been recommended by Chinese health practitioners to increase the libido and eradicate fatigue. These "yang" foods stimulate the qi, emanate heat, and increase energy levels. Diet can have a significant influence on sexual desire and behavior. Meat, fish, shellfish, eggs, salt, spices, onions, and garlic are all very yang and can act as aphrodisiacs. Animal products, especially meat and seafood, contain uric acid, which stimulates the genital mucous membranes and triggers sexual arousal. Traditional Chinese Medicine (TCM) recommends shrimp, Chinese chive, beef, lamb, walnuts, carrots, rice, royal jelly, and lycium fruit for igniting libido and increasing sexual desire.

Herbal Aphrodisiacs

Some classic Chinese herbs used for many centuries to enhance health, sexual desire, libido, and passion include:

* *Cordyceps sinensis* (dong chong xia cao), a Chinese fungus energy tonic and aphrodisiac.

* Dong quai (Chinese angelica), a.k.a. "female ginseng."
* Gecko (ge jie)—like deer horn, this regenerative creature has been used in traditional Chinese medicine for millennia to rev up the sex drive. Usually baked and ground into a powder.
* Ginger.
* Green and white tea.
* Lycium fruit (gou qi zi)—used in sexual tonics for more than 2,500 years, and said to promote longevity, physical strength, and sexual potency.
* Nan bao, an energy herb for men.
* *Panax* ginseng (ren shen).
* Pilose deer horn/antler (lu rong), lightly baked and ground into a powder, and taken with liquid or a small amount of Chinese wine.
* Saw palmetto (for men).
* Wu ji bai feng wan, an anti-fatigue patent herb for women.
* Yin yang huo, a.k.a. *Epimedium* or "horny goatweed" (no, I'm not kidding!)—the number-one choice to boost both male and female libido.
* Yohimbe (for men).

Note: While Chinese herbs have been used safely for millenniums, you should discuss the use of these or any other herbs with your doctor, especially if you are taking medication or have other health conditions.

Sign-Specific Seduction

Fantasy is a critical element of sexual fulfillment and lovemaking. Each of the 12 Chinese Zodiac signs has their own sexual "mind garden" that can be cultivated to yield a very delicious harvest! Here are some suggestions for the seduction of, and likely turn-ons for, each sign:

The Rat—a sprinter and quick out of the gate in romance.

Needs: reassurance, exploration.

Hates: criticism, feeling lost in a crowd.

Turn-ons: phone sex, erotic talk.

The Ox—slow and sure, this is the marathon lover of the Zodiac.

Needs: respect, security.

Hates: insubordination.

Turn-ons: scented candles, oils, flowers.

The Tiger—conquest is the name of this sign's game.

Needs: adventure, passion.

Hates: routine, ingratitude.

Turn-ons: full body massage.

The Rabbit—refinement and subtlety are this sign's aphrodisiacs.

Needs: serenity, freedom.

Hates: unpleasantness, entrapment.

Turn-ons: romantic dinners, slow seduction.

The Dragon—this dramatic actor on the stage of life likes to impress.

Needs: admiration, self-expression.

Hates: small or cramped spaces, weakness.

Turn-ons: thunderstorms, movies, the theatre.

The Snake—seduction, secrets, and savvy are this sign's charms.

Needs: privacy.

Hates: crass or boorish people.

Turn-ons: music, secrets.

The Horse—a friendly and expressive lover, with a strong need for acknowledgment.

Needs: communication.

Hates: sticks-in-the-mud, party poopers.

Turn-ons: gourmet food, fine wine, travel.

The Goat—floating from one romantic cloud to another, this is the artistic love poet of the Zodiac.

Needs: flexibility, security.

Hates: responsibility, hard decisions.

Turn-ons: the oceanfront, secluded beaches, lakes.

The Monkey—social, witty, and complicated, this sign thrives with a calm, intuitive lover.

Needs: versatility.

Hates: humorless people, control.

Turn-ons: Las Vegas, Atlantic City, casinos.

The Rooster—rigid and meticulous, this sign is a perfectionist in the art of lovemaking.

Needs: attention, control, attractive clothing.

Hates: sloth, slowness.

Turn-ons: spanking, costumes, role playing.

The Dog—trust and emotional attachment is always a serious business with this sign.

Needs: a confidante, loyalty.

Hates: cruelty, unfairness.

Turn-ons: firesides, fur rugs, log cabins.

The Pig—loyal, honest, and sensual, and an easygoing, unselfish lover, this sign needs large amounts of affection.

Needs: affection, physical love.

Hates: competition, breaking the rules.

Turn-ons: Jacuzzis, hot tubs, bubble baths.

PART III

BODY CONNECTIONS

With the love of beauty as his constant joy,
he decides to visit his lover's chambers.

—Songs of Chu

CHAPTER 14

鼠牛虎兔龍蛇馬羊猴鷄犬猪

"CHING QI"—
CHANNELING RAW SEXUAL ENERGY

THE MOST ANCIENT FORMS OF SEXUALITY are those of the Taoist arts and tantra. Both tantra (India) and Taoism (China) are concerned with balancing the masculine and feminine energies. Taoist practice knows this as the yin and yang energies, while Tantric practice refers to this as Shakti and Shiva. Both being pioneers in spiritual sexuality, they share a common goal of uniting the physical with the spiritual. However, Taoist beliefs regarding *ching qi* (raw sexual energy) differ from those of its tantric cousin. Tantric sexual practice seeks to channel the ching qi from the genital root chakra up to the brain; Taoist sexual practice goes a step further and seeks to bring this energy back down to its point of origin. This balances the sexual energy and creates a complete cycle or "sexual circuit." Taoist sexual cultivation seeks to unite the "three treasures" of ching (sexual energy), qi (life force, breath), and shen (spiritual and mental energy). With plentiful ching, the life qi thrives and is able to balance the shen. For the Chinese, circulating life-giving qi by means of sex was the path to good health and happiness.

Exchanging sexual qi with a partner during sex works best when we are spiritually and mentally in tune with each other. One of the best ways to achieve this is for the woman to sit facing her man on his lap so that his hardened penis can enter her vagina. She may want to wrap her legs around his waist or he may wish to support her using his arms around her back or waist. This way, the two lovers can make eye contact with each other as they consciously project love and positive sexual energy toward each other.

Deep kissing is another ideal way to complete the sexual "qi circuit." While in the face-to-face deep affinity position described previously, the lovers also make contact with each others' mouth and tongue. This erotic kissing circulates healthy qi throughout their bodies and creates a complete sexual circuit. When you do this, close your eyes and picture a warm energy beginning at the base of your genitals, rising up to your head, then back down again through your partner's body, making a full circle.

Jade

Jade or jadeite has enjoyed a place of honor in Chinese civilization since the dawn of history. This "divine stone" has graced holy altars, been fashioned into exquisite jewelry, and was said to have spiritual and magical qualities. Technically classified as a gem, the ancient Chinese held this stone in high esteem. With a natural hardness almost as tough as the diamond, jade has long been a favorite material for purposes from the mystical to the mundane. First used for making tools, jade soon developed medical, social, and religious significance. For millennia, jade has been revered for its beauty and durability, and has been viewed as a symbol of power.

In China, the mystique surrounding jade is evident in ancient sexual terminology as well as in classical writings, such as the *Art of the Jade Bedchamber*. It was also frequently used as an adjective, as in "jade stem," the ancient Chinese term for a man's penis. The use of jade as a metaphor indicated that it was his most prized possession. For thousands of years, the Chinese have called it the "stone of China," believing it to bring protection, sexual virility, and peace of mind. Nephrite, also known as chen yu or "true jade," is the oldest, softest, and most common type of jade. It was used in ancient carvings, some of which have been dated at more than 4,000 years old.

The value of the stone depends on its color, texture, and translucency. The most sought-after and highest quality jade is a uniform, deep emerald green with almost total translucency, known as "Imperial" or "old mine" jade. It is so exquisite and rare that its value rivals the highest grade emeralds. Once owned solely by emperors, Jade remains prized in China above all other gemstones. Jade has retained its value over the centuries and remains the ultimate symbol of virtue and beauty. It is aptly dubbed "the concentrated essence of love."

Sexual Terminology

In the colorful Chinese tradition of combining utility with poetry, the mundane with the esoteric, the ancients' sexual glossary was both entertaining and illuminating. Here are some of the most frequently used terms and their meanings.

* Jade stem—penis or ambassador.
* Jade gate—vagina or heavenly palace.
* Red lotus peak—lips.
* Twin white peaks—breasts.
* Flowery pool—mouth.
* White tiger's cave or jade vein—vulva.
* Palace of yin—uterus.
* Inner door—cervix.
* Jade fluid—saliva.
* Flood of yin tide—female orgasm.
* Surrendering—male orgasm.
* Yu heng—penis.
* Male ching—semen.
* Pearl on the jade step—clitoris.
* Clouds and rain—sexual intercourse.
* Sexual tigress—a female Taoist who sought to retain youth, perfect physical restoration, and attain enlightenment through specific sexual practices and disciplines.
* Courtesan—an intelligent, respected, and highly educated woman who was a professional companion. Her company was a sign of high social standing and she was well-versed in poetry and writing, as well as in the Tao of love.
* Consort—a woman of exceptional charm and great beauty who would be the ancient equivalent of a modern man's mistress. She lived a comfortable, sequestered life.

* Concubine—not to be confused with a prostitute, she was a second wife to a man and enjoyed financial and emotional support in exchange for giving him children and sexual enjoyment.

* Jade dragon—a man who co-partnered with the sexual tigress to practice and perfect physical restoration and enlightenment through sexuality. (They engaged in a long-term relationship of between three and nine years, to be evaluated after three years to see if both parties wished to continue their intimate relationship.)

* Green dragon—a man whose only purpose was to give the sexual tigress sexual pleasure, variety, and vital sexual yang qi.

The Eight Jade Stems and Their Attainments

The ancient Chinese were somewhat obsessed with both predicting the future and assigning archetypal profile to everything, and the penis was no exception. The *Su Nu Miao Lun*, an ancient Taoist sexual manuscript, describes the four yang "attainments" and the eight "archetypes" of jade stems (penises).

The four yang attainments:

* Lengthening—early arousal
* Dilation—firming but not fully erect
* Hardening—full erection, orgasms possible
* Flash—point of ejaculation

The male yang (+) energy has two separate and distinct energies: orgasm and ejaculation. Ejaculation is a muscle spasm that originates at the base of the spine and releases semen. Orgasm is the exquisite pleasure experienced that originates in the brain. Most men believe orgasm and ejaculation to be one and the same, but Eastern teachings actually separate the two.

Learning to slow down, relax his breathing, and draw the sexual energy within will keep a man in the hardening stage without going over the edge to the ejaculatory or flash point stage. It is by staying within this hardening stage that a man can experience multiple orgasms and take control of his lovemaking experience. Practicing this can result in the man experiencing as many orgasms as he desires until his partner is satisfied or until he decides to ejaculate.

The eight jade stems:

* The low valley stem—3″ × 7″, short and very thick (youthful yang +). This type of penis is quick to become aroused but slow to climax. This stem represents the mouth—its owner is a verbally seductive smooth talker and has many sexual partners. The Earth-ruled period of Indian summer is his peak time for romance.

* The earthly stem—4″ × 3″, short and thin (absolute yin -). This type of penis can be slow to become aroused but responds nicely if stimulated. This stem represents the digestive system—its owner is a nurturer, very giving and quick to become involved. The Water-ruled period of winter is his peak time for romance.

* The thunder stem—5″ × 5″, medium and medium (mature yang +). This type of penis resembles a skyrocket as it is quickly aroused but rapidly dissipates. This stem represents the feet—its owner is physically active, seeks quick stimulation and resolution, and may make promises in the heat of passion that he later has trouble fulfilling. The Fire-ruled period of summer is his peak time for romance.

* The wind stem—6″ × 3″, long and thin (aged yin -). This type of penis has staying power and seeks extended and intense stimulation. This stem represents the upper thighs—its owner seeks to be in close physical proximity with women but may consider relationships closer than they really are. The Wood-ruled period of early spring is his peak time for romance.

* The water stem—6″ × 4″, long and medium thick (medium yin -). This type of penis is "hard to read" and mysterious, and prefers slower, extended sex. This stem represents the auditory system—its owner is a listener, which is how he endears himself to women. The Wood-ruled period of spring is his peak time for romance.

* The fire stem—7″ × 5″, very long and medium thick (medium yang +). This type of penis needs very little stimulation and can have trouble lasting as long as he and his lover would like. This stem represents the eyes—its owner's gaze is intense and sensual, which is how he attracts women. The

Metal-ruled period of late fall is his peak time for romance.

* The mountain stem— 8″ × 5″, extremely long with medium thickness (youthful yin -). This type of penis seeks frequent stimulation, has staying power, and is slow to climax. This stem represents the hands—its owner is helpful and impassioned, and enmeshed with his lover. The Water-ruled period of winter is his peak time for romance.

* The heavenly jade stem—8″-plus × 7″, extremely long with greatest thickness (ultimate yang +). This type of penis seeks intense and frequent encounters and is bold and assertive. This stem represents the face—its owner is a smiling charmer, and uses his expression to seduce. The Fire-ruled period of summer is his peak time for romance.

The Three Jade Gates and Their Stages

The female yin (-) energy is rejuvenated after each monthly cycle. A woman's body uses her orgasm to nourish her body and stimulate vital life qi. She is the receiver (yin) of her partner's (yang) qi. In ancient times the woman's vagina was referred to as her "jade gate"; there were three types of jade gates and three stages of arousal.

The three female "waters" or stages:

* Lubrication
* Orgasm
* Ejaculation (originating from what is known as the "G-spot," and manifest as abundant vaginal fluid or an actual spray of liquid upon orgasm)

The three jade gates:

* The jade door—a short vagina no more than five inches long, usually found in women of small stature.
* The jade gate—a medium vagina seven inches long, usually found in women of medium stature with wider hips.
* The jade courtyard—a long vagina of 10 inches or more, usually found in women of larger stature with ample breasts and proportions.

Stem and gate size and compatibility:

* Jade gate (medium) goes with the thunder, wind, water, or fire jade stems.
* Jade courtyard (large) goes with the two "jade hammers"— the mountain or heavenly jade stems.

Birth and Conception

In the Eastern tradition, sex for the purpose of generating a new body for a soul to inhabit is regarded as a creative, sacred act. The following chart is believed to have been buried in a tomb near Beijing for almost 700 years (the original is now in the Beijing Institute of Science). By cross-referencing the month a child was conceived with the age of the mother at conception, the sex of the child may be determined. For those couples wishing to conceive, this chart has been estimated to be between 93 and 99 percent accurate.

According to this ancient data, the best chances for a boy occur when the mother conceives in July and she is 18, 20, 30, or 42. The best chances for a girl occur when the mother conceives in April and she is 21, 22, or 29. Also, a boy is 54 percent more likely to be born in general. Have fun with this one!

AGE AT CONCEPTION	Month of Conception												Stats	
	J	F	M	A	M	J	J	A	S	O	N	D	F	M
18	Fem	Mal	Fem	Mal	Mal	Mal	Mal	Mal	Mal	Mal	Mal	Mal	17%	83%
19	Mal	Fem	Mal	Fem	Fem	Mal	Mal	Fem	Mal	Mal	Fem	Fem	50%	50%
20	Fem	Mal	Fem	Mal	Mal	Mal	Mal	Mal	Mal	Fem	Mal	Mal	25%	75%
21	Mal	Fem	Fem	Fem	Fem	Fem	Fem	Fem	Fem	Fem	Fem	Fem	92%	8%
22	Fem	Mal	Mal	Fem	Mal	Fem	Fem	Fem	Fem	Fem	Fem	Fem	67%	33%
23	Mal	Mal	Mal	Fem	Mal	Mal	Fem	Fem	Fem	Mal	Mal	Fem	42%	58%
24	Mal	Fem	Fem	Mal	Mal	Fem	Mal	Fem	Mal	Mal	Fem	Mal	42%	58%
25	Fem	Mal	Fem	Mal	Fem	Mal	Fem	Mal	Fem	Mal	Mal	Mal	42%	58%
26	Mal	Mal	Mal	Mal	Mal	Fem	Mal	Fem	Fem	Fem	Fem	Fem	42%	58%
27	Fem	Fem	Mal	Mal	Fem	Mal	Fem	Fem	Fem	Fem	Mal	Mal	50%	50%
28	Mal	Mal	Mal	Fem	Fem	Mal	Mal	Mal	Fem	Fem	Fem	Fem	50%	50%
29	Fem	Mal	Fem	Fem	Mal	Fem	Fem	Mal	Fem	Mal	Mal	Fem	67%	33%
30	Mal	Mal	Fem	Mal	Fem	Mal	Mal	Fem	Mal	Fem	Mal	Mal	17%	83%
31	Mal	Mal	Mal	Mal	Fem	Fem	Mal	Mal	Mal	Mal	Fem	Fem	50%	50%
32	Mal	Fem	Fem	Mal	Fem	Mal	Mal	Fem	Mal	Mal	Fem	Mal	42%	58%

AGE AT CONCEPTION	Month of Conception												Stats	
	J	F	M	A	M	J	J	A	S	O	N	D	F	M
33	Fem	Mal	Mal	Fem	Fem	Mal	Fem	Mal	Fem	Mal	Mal	Fem	50%	50%
34	Mal	Mal	Fem	Fem	Mal	Fem	Mal	Mal	Fem	Mal	Fem	Fem	50%	50%
35	Mal	Fem	Mal	Fem	Mal	Fem	Mal	Fem	Mal	Mal	Fem	Mal	42%	58%
36	Mal	Fem	Mal	Mal	Fem	Fem	Mal	Fem	Fem	Fem	Fem	Fem	50%	50%
37	Fem	Fem	Mal	Fem	Fem	Mal	Mal	Mal	Fem	Mal	Mal	Mal	58%	42%
38	Mal	Mal	Fem	Fem	Fem	Fem	Fem	Mal	Fem	Fem	Mal	Fem	58%	42%
39	Fem	Fem	Mal	Fem	Fem	Mal	Mal	Fem	Mal	Mal	Fem	Mal	58%	42%
40	Mal	Mal	Mal	Fem	Mal	Mal	Mal	Fem	Mal	Fem	Fem	Mal	42%	58%
41	Fem	Fem	Mal	Fem	Mal	Fem	Fem	Fem	Fem	Fem	Mal	Fem	50%	50%
42	Mal	Fem	Fem	Mal	Mal	Mal	Mal	Mal	Fem	Mal	Fem	Mal	33%	67%
43	Fem	Fem	Fem	Fem	Mal	Mal	Mal	Fem	Fem	Fem	Mal	Mal	50%	50%
44	Mal	Mal	Fem	Fem	Mal	Fem	Mal	Mal	Fem	Mal	Fem	Mal	50%	50%
45	Fem	Mal	Fem	Mal	Fem	Fem	Mal	Fem	Mal	Fem	Mal	Fem	58%	42%
Total F	43%	43%	50%	57%	43%	54%	36%	54%	54%	43%	54%	50%	46%	
Total M	57%	57%	50%	43%	57%	46%	64%	46%	46%	57%	46%	50%		54%

CHAPTER 15

鼠牛虎兔龍蛇馬羊猴鷄犬猪

Sizzling Sex in the Taoist Tradition

One must directly face their sexuality, or they will never discover their spirituality; through physical spirit we find the path to heavenly spirit. Examine what created you to find what will immortalize you.

—Manual of the White Tigress

Ejaculation Control and Longevity

Some time between 2697 and 2598 B.C.E., the Yellow Emperor, Huang Ti, sought the advice of Su Nu Ching (the plain girl). It is said that the emperor's health was deteriorating from excess and overindulgence in sex. The plain girl taught the emperor the secrets of restoring his vitality, developing his sexual energy, and how to better address the needs of a woman. To balance the yin/yang aspect of sexuality and to restore his health, she taught that it was important for him to have infrequent ejaculations but to bring his female partner frequently to orgasm. She stressed the importance of using sexual techniques for mental and spiritual benefit. One of the most important texts on sexual techniques, *The Art of the Bedchamber*, encouraged prolonged sexual intercourse for the man to obtain more nourishment from the female yin essence before giving up his own yang essence through ejaculation.

As mentioned in the previous chapter, the male yang (+) sexual energy has two separate energies—orgasm and ejaculation. Ejaculation is a muscle spasm that originates at the base of the spine and releases semen, while orgasm is the exquisite pleasure experienced that originates in the brain. Most Western men believe that these are the same thing, but Taoist teachings separate the two. It is not uncommon for young males to masturbate to orgasm before ejaculation is physically possible for them, but during adolescence orgasm and the act of ejaculation become merged. This prevents many men from enjoying multiple orgasms, preserving their ching, and developing erectile staying power.

Ejaculation Control

There are several effective techniques that a man can use to "cool down" and let his desire subside in order to prolong intercourse. One of these techniques involves placing the index finger and thumb around the base of the erect penal shaft and applying firm pressure against the underside of the lower part of the penis. The head of the penis is then gently squeezed between the index finger and thumb of the other hand until the urge to ejaculate has subsided.

Another practice, called the "jen mo" technique, is also used to gain physical control of ejaculation in order to prolong the sexual act and to recirculate the man's vital sexual energies up to his brain and throughout his body. In this technique, mild to moderate pressure is applied to the area between the testicles and the anus (the jen mo point) when ejaculation is near, thus diminishing the urge to ejaculate and allowing intercourse to continue.

While the male *loses* energy during the sex act and subsequent ejaculation, the female *gains* energy by receiving qi from the man. Therefore Taoist sexual doctrine teaches the value of a man's semen as a source of vitality and thus promotes semen conservation. However, this should *not* be interpreted to mean that a man's semen is so essential to health and longevity that ejaculation must be avoided or conserved to excess. These teachings were intended to assist each man in finding the right frequency of ejaculation to suit his age and physical condition. Complete abstinence is as harmful to a man's health as excess. Each individual must find his own healthy balance and be guided by common sense and moderation. (It must be said here that while the traditional Taoist ejaculation control methods are effective and promote vitality, it is perfectly acceptable for a man to choose to orgasm and ejaculate together. Even the exhaustion he feels after ejaculation is not a bad thing if it relieves his stress and relaxes his body.)

As women have their monthly cycles, so also do men experience their own biological cycles. According to ancient Taoist writings, the time interval between ejaculations helped a man regain lost energy and sexual ching (although he was advised to have sexual relations as frequently as possible during this time). Master Tsu Hse, an early founder of Taoist medicine who lived during the Sui Dynasty (581-618 c.e.), advised the following general guidelines regarding ejaculation frequency.

For healthy males in **good condition** (sheng qi):

> 15-20 years old—once a day
> 20-30 years old—every 2 days
> 30-40 years old—every 3 days
> 40-50 years old—every 4 days
> 50-60 years old—every 5 days
> 60-70 years old—every 10 days
> 70-80 years old—every 20 days
> 80-90 years old—every 40 days

For males in **average** condition (si qi):

> 15-20 years old—every 3 days
> 20-30 years old—every 5 days
> 30-40 years old—every 6 days
> 40-50 years old—every 8 days
> 50-60 years old—every 10 days
> 60-70 years old—every 20 days
> 70-80 years old—every 30 days
> 80-90 years old—every 80 days

For males in **poor** condition (sha qi):

> 15-20 years old—every 5 days
> 20-30 years old—every 7 days
> 30-40 years old—every 9 days
> 40-50 years old—every 12 days
> 50-60 years old—every 15 days
> 60-70 years old—every 30 days

70-80 years old—every 50 days

80-90 years old—no ejaculations are advised

There are also minimum ejaculation recommendations by age:

For a healthy male 20 years old—at least every 4 days

For a health male 40 year old—at least every 16 days

For a healthy male 60 years old—at least every 30 days

Each man is unique and must discover his own bodily rhythms. Healthy, balanced sex is not about the destination of ejaculation, but part of a longer sexual journey designed to nurture love, spirituality, and to exchange bodily yin and yang energies.

White Tigers and Jade Dragons

There was a sect of female Taoist masters who specialized in the act of love. These "white tigresses" were a secret sect of very disciplined and skilled women who undertook sexual and spiritual practices (especially receiving a man's yang ching qi essence through oral sex) to maintain their beauty and youthfulness, and to eventually attain enlightenment and immortality. The tigress devoted herself to certain sexual practices handed down through the lineage of Hsi Wang Mu, or "Western Royal Mother," to realize her full feminine potential through her sexuality. Typically she lived for a nine year period with her "jade dragon," who was her protector, benefactor, best friend, and lover. He provided her with the financial and emotional support necessary for her to practice her sexual craft. Their relationship was built upon being co-partners in the sexual restorative process, with mutual enlightenment as the ultimate goal. Men who desired to be jade dragons would have to find a fledgling white tigress who would agree to this arrangement. Many times he would be older so that he would be emotionally mature and free from jealousy, and in a better position to support her.

The first three years of the relationship was the "restoration period," devoted to refining the tigress' ching (sexual energy). The second three-year period was the woman's "preservation period," when she would accumulate life breath or qi. The last three years was the "refinement period," when the woman would perfect her shen (spiritual consciousness). The union was evaluated after the first three years to determine if each partner wished to continue.

The white tigress had five distinct physical characteristics that marked her as such:

* Extremely long, straight hair (representing health and femininity).
* A small waist (to arouse passion).
* Reddened lips (emphasizing her oral skills).
* Long painted fingernails.
* A shaved pubic area (emphasizing her youth).

Sizzling Sex in the Taoist Tradition

In ancient times, young men were taught certain behaviors and techniques to seduce a woman and help ensure a harmonious love life. According to these teachings, a superior lover should begin by making contact with his partner's fingertips using his middle finger. Using his hands he slowly moves up her arm to the shoulders where he gently caresses her. He strokes the backs of her hands with his middle, index, and ring fingers, moving to her palms using small circular movements. He then uses his fingers to trace up her inner arms to her shoulders once again.

Her lover then moves down to her feet and touches the tips of her toes moving up her foot and leg along her inner thigh until he reaches her *mons pubis* (mound of Venus). After caressing her hands and feet, he draws her to him in a gentle hug while kissing first her neck then her forehead. He continues caressing, licking, and kissing her lips, neck, and breasts. He returns once again to kiss her earlobes, and moves to the more erogenous zones such as her lower back, abdomen, buttocks, and inner thighs. He is then free to kiss or lick her most sensitive areas such as the vaginal lips and clitoris. Once her lover has kissed or caressed every part of her body, she is then properly prepared for sexual activity or intercourse.

CHAPTER 16

鼠牛虎兔龍蛇馬羊猴雞犬猪

Sexual Styles: The Tame, the Tawdry, and— Sometimes—the Taboo

As the cultural revolution came to the fore in China, sex became a taboo subject. Most modern-day Chinese are still very conservative about sex, and have no idea that their ancestors were so open about sexuality. China has enjoyed a long history of relishing sex, and it is an inseparable part of the culture. There was a time when the topic was not considered vulgar or obscene, and people were encouraged to adopt a scientific, natural, and healthy view about it. The Museum of Ancient Chinese Sexual Culture in Tongli, Jiangsu China, houses thousands of sexual artifacts and antiquities. Its contents are a confirmation that people were quite open about sex before the Tang Dynasty. Various taboos started to surface during the middle of the Song Dynasty, and to this day, a conflict exists between openness and the unutterable.

There exists an erroneous notion that the Chinese were misogynistic regarding women and sexuality. With the exception of the dark and twisted period in history where foot binding and other warped practices were briefly in vogue, this was never practiced in the Tao of love. In fact, the 7th-century physician and alchemist, Li T'ung Hsuan, admonished that "a man must wait for his partner to be satisfied...every time." If this could not be accomplished, Hsuan taught that the man had "much room for improvement."

There is also the misapprehension that Chinese sexuality is merely a set of methods, devoid of spontaneity and emotion. Nothing could be farther from the truth! Ancient Taoist sexual techniques are only one part of the whole experience that seeks to combine the qi (life force) with the ching (sexual energy).

Masturbation in Ancient China

The Chinese view male and female self-gratification quite differently. The female yin (-) energy is abundant and recharged after each monthly lunar cycle. The woman's body uses the orgasm to nourish her own body and recirculate vital life qi; none of her energy is lost as a result of her orgasm. This stands in contrast to the man's sexual yang (+) energy, which is finite and quickly becomes depleted upon ejaculation. Taoist tradition discouraged excessive masturbation not because of moral implications, but rather because of its disturbance of the yin/yang balance. According to Taoist teaching, the more frequently a man has an orgasm without ejaculating, the more sexual energy he has available (see Chapter 15). For a man, orgasms are energy-producing while ejaculation is depleting.

Female Masturbation

Understanding the reflex zones of the female vagina is important in any discussion of female masturbation. The outer part of the female vaginal vault corresponds to the organs of the kidneys and bladder, and the area just behind this corresponds to the liver and gallbladder. The middle vaginal area corresponds to the digestive and pancreatic systems, with the lungs and intestines located at the upper vaginal vault area. The cervix at the end of the vagina corresponds to the heart and circulatory systems.

According to ancient wisdom, focusing on the clitoris (a common occurrence), to the exclusion of intercourse (the jade stem entering the jade gate), is said to neglect the woman's "jade gate." When stimulation of the vital internal organs via the reflex zones is absent, weakness of the bladder, retention of fluids, or female weight gain may be the result. The ideal scenario is combining the two in perfect yin/yang balance. The "valley proper" position, in which the woman stimulates her clitoris while her partner penetrates her (see Chapter 29), is a pleasurable and balanced solution.

Male Masturbation

Similar to the vagina, the penis also has its own correspondences to the vital internal organs. The head and tip of the penis is the reflex point for the heart and lungs. Concentration on this one area during masturbation, to the exclusion of others, can create an imbalance by overstimulating the cardio-pulmonary system. This is why a man should include the entire penal shaft during self-pleasuring. As stated previously, the male yang (+) energy has two discrete expressions—orgasm and ejaculation—and Eastern teachings categorize the two activities as separate and distinct. In the Taoist tradition, when a man masturbates and does not indiscriminately ejaculate, he preserves his vital life force and practices the greatest respect for his spirit, his mind, and his body.

Adult Toys

Vibrators and other modern electric or battery operated adult "toys" are touted by many as an ideal supplement either for self-pleasuring or for use with a partner. However, vibrators are not an ideal choice for female clitoral stimulation. They can desensitize the organ and micro-scar delicate tissue, which can result in the woman requiring increasingly greater clitoral pressure and stimulation to achieve orgasm. In the Taoist tradition, it is suggested that a woman should not use anything rougher on her clitoris for self-pleasuring than the gentle touch of the tip of her finger.

Voyeurism

Voyeurism can be used to heighten a man's desire and rev up a flagging libido. The yang brain is visually oriented and watching the sexual act is a recipe for an explosive orgasm. If the man so chooses, he may elect not to ejaculate, directing his intense sexual ching energy up along his spine and to his brain instead. (If you engage in this activity, just be sure to keep it between consenting adults.)

Spanking

If both parties are amenable, a lover may take their partner over their lap and spank their buttocks hard enough for them to turn just slightly red, awakening and reviving the nerve endings. This "dry bath," or "patting" as the Taoists call it, is used in qi gong exercises to bring blood flow into various body parts. However, the rule is that spanking can never be done unless requested. In the *Secrets of the White Tigress* sexual training manual, there are many examples of a woman requesting her man to playfully "discipline" her after he secretly and voyeuristically watches her engage in sexual acts with another man (a green dragon) of her choice. The green dragon's purpose was purely to give life yang force through oral sex to the tigress.

Exhibitionism

Men enjoy showing off their virility to women, just as women enjoy teasing and taunting a man into sexual intoxication. The quality and quantity of a man's semen is an external sign of his manhood and a confirmation of the woman's desirability. The white tigress would attract green dragons through a subtle and sophisticated exhibitionism.

From the explicit imagery of 200 B.C.E. tomb tiles, to the erotic novel *Ching Ping Mei*, the ménage a trois was not an unusual kind of sexuality in ancient times. These ancient texts and pictures depict a very different feeling about privacy—in one such picture, you can see a servant helping a couple have sex in a chair (which was also very popular in China).

Anal Sex

The kundalini gland, or hui yin ("returning yin") spot, is located two or three finger widths deep inside the anus. This is where the Taoist thought the ching (sexual essence) and qi (life force) joined to rise up to the brain via the spine, culminating in spiritual enlightenment. Inserting a lubricated finger into the anus (with the palm facing downward) and gently massaging or tapping this area is known to produce rock hard erections in some men and great pleasure in some women. In anal sex, only the penile head is allowed to penetrate the anus very gently and gradually, and ejaculation is not allowed.

Shaving

One of the ways the ancients would renew and revitalize their sexual youthfulness was through shaving of the genitals. Although both men and women would shave the pubic area, shaving of the *mons pubis* was one of the five signs of a "white tigress." While a prickly proposition for many women to consider, it was at one time a mainstay for many Chinese women.

Taboos

Curiously enough, the ancient Chinese sexual taboos are not so much related to specific practices and positions as they are health- and timing-related.

Here is a list of traditional sexual no-no's:

* Sexual relations when fatigued, disinterested, or in a state of anger.

* Sex when ill (apparently, being "love sick" isn't a good idea).

* Sex right after a meal (especially during the Horse-ruled hours of 11 a.m. to 1 p.m., and the Pig-ruled hours of 9 p.m. to 11 p.m.).

* Sex directly following male urination.

* Sex right after an operation or acupuncture treatment.

* Sex while intoxicated.

* Sex in temples, cemeteries, or churches.

* Sex during war or other tumultuous and fearful periods.

* Sex when traveling on a journey via airplane or ship (upsets endocrine system).

* Sex on the summer solstice (when yang turns to yin) or winter solstice (when yin turns to yang), or during solar/lunar eclipses.

Traditionally auspicious times for sex:

* Two weeks before and one week after the woman's menstrual period.

* Early morning hours ruled by the Rabbit (Mao), between 5 a.m. and 7 a.m.

* Early evening hours ruled by the Dog (Xu), between 7 p.m. and 9 p.m.

CHAPTER 17

鼠牛虎兔龍蛇馬羊猴鷄犬猪

RANDY RAT

Jan 31, 1900 to Feb 18, 1901: Metal Rat
Feb 18, 1912 to Feb 5, 1913: Water Rat
Feb 5, 1924 to Jan 24, 1925: Wood Rat
Jan 24, 1936 to Feb 10, 1937: Fire Rat
Feb 10, 1948 to Jan 28, 1949: Earth Rat
Jan 28, 1960 to Feb 14, 1961: Metal Rat
Feb 15, 1972 to Feb 2, 1973: Water Rat
Feb 2, 1984 to Feb 19, 1985: Wood Rat
Feb 19, 1996 to Feb 6, 1997: Fire Rat
Feb 7, 2008 to Jan 25, 2009: Earth Rat
Needs: reassurance
Hates: being alone
Turn-ons: youth, innocence
Turnoffs: detached partners

The socially adept Rat possesses charisma, intelligence, and the ability to charm the pants off of just about anybody—literally. Their sexual repertoire is as varied as their eclectic interests. Once aroused, Rats want to "get down to business," and tend to be quick starters sprinting out of the love gate.

They need a sexual partner who is mentally bright, willing to listen to and converse with them, and who is just a tad kinky. Talkative Rats live in a romantic world of their own and enjoy a rich fantasy life. High-strung, curious, and ever alert to sexual opportunity, Rats need to make an emotional connection with their potential lover. They rule the concealed and stealthy midnight hours of secrets and delicious debauchery.

If your man was born into a Rat year:

Whether your Rat is a professor or a playboy, an energetic, happy aura in a female is irresistible to him. This is a man who is attracted to a clean, robust, athletic look, generally slim but not necessarily skinny. A tousled, casual appearance is just fine with him. His sexual preferences are deeply rooted in his psychology. This is a man who seeks his twin soul—a sisterly type who is an accomplice, a best friend, and someone intimately familiar with his background and desires. Head games, playing hard to get, and other coquettish tricks on the part of his lover will frustrate this high-strung man. He has little patience with women who take this approach.

The woman of his fantasies is young, slim, and even somewhat androgynous. She has a playful demeanor, yet is intelligent enough to engage him in interesting conversation. She is young and rather inexperienced (he'll have to teach her, of course!), and shy about the ways of the world. Svengali, Don Juan, and Casanova all rolled into one charmer of a man— that's our Rat!

Your Rat lover thinks of sex much like an amusement park where he is free to run from one ride to the next. Many times, this taste for sexual variety can cause friction in the fidelity department. Similar to his Dragon brother, the Rat male also needs to feel admired. Much of his sexuality is based on the thrill of the chase and attracting various "audiences." There can be a tendency toward sexual addictions of every description and a troublesome addiction to the chase phase in romance. With a Rat, sexual exploration and need for freedom are to be expected even in marriage, so the sexual partner of this man must stay on her toes. It is important that she demand absolute sexual honesty from her Rat and let him know upfront that she will not tolerate any flirting or indiscretions.

Despite his youthful, boyish good looks, the Rat man can be self-centered sexually. Since he likes to "get down to business" as quickly as possible, foreplay isn't his strong suit. In addition, he tends to be fixed and set on the goal of ejaculation. The holy grail for this lover is to s-l-o-w down, listen to his partner's body language, and enjoy the "journey" more. This is a man who must consciously choose more leisurely and spontaneous lovemaking. He should practice letting his erection decrease a bit before he reaches the point of no return, in order to experience a brief "cool down" period. Once this technique is successfully mastered, he will draw more energy into his own body (and have a happier partner as well).

The good news is that these lovers are direct and outspoken in their desires and preferences, so you won't ever be playing a guessing game. The Rat man has an innocent frankness about him—he intends to have fun in bed, and a good laugh with his partner is a huge turn-on. Passion and sensitivity are not his strong points, but laughter and fun are aphrodisiacs for this cerebral lover.

If your woman was born into a Rat year:

It is after sunset, during the midnight hours, that the Rat woman comes alive with numerous acquaintances, lively discussion, and intensely romantic interludes. She values companionship and love more than anything else. This is an ardent lover who easily expresses the physical side of her love. This deeply emotional soul yearns for affection and sincere attention. To love and to be understood are as vital to her as breathing. She needs a partner to cherish as well as one who cherishes her in return.

Her passion for knowledge, love of travel, and hunger for new experiences make the Rat female extremely enticing. Usually of small or slight frame and stature, the Rat woman is the "tiny mouse" of the Eastern Zodiac. Frail, sensitive to a myriad of environmental insults, and prone to delicate health, the Rat female is the type of woman men love to rescue. She will routinely be found atop a white horse beside her current knight in shining armor, who is always ready to slay a beast for her. Her biggest hurdle is her own body image, which her critical nature just can't help judging ruthlessly. The saying "a woman can neither be too rich nor too thin" was most assuredly authored by a female Rat.

Rat girls fall in love easily and are prone to infatuations. Freedom-loving, likable, and a natural philanderer, the Rat woman enjoys being in love. One of her difficulties is that she always wants more. She has this nagging feeling there could be something more exciting just around the corner. It takes a strong love to hold her!

Exchanging and communicating are the priorities of a Rat woman, and conversing in the bedroom is an absolute necessity. She ignores social taboos and doesn't hesitate to tackle the most intimate or controversial subjects. By encouraging her freedom of expression, you'll strengthen your bonds with her. Those who love a Rat female should be warned that she's a natural flirt. She treasures her personal freedom above everything (and everyone) else, so she will not tolerate your jealousy or possessiveness regarding her flirtations. So, be ready to be patient and understanding when you see her playing the flirt before your eyes. Be indulgent, and remember that home and family are actually the things that count the most to her.

The hidden elemental stem in the Rat year branch is Water, and this fluidity shows up in the Rat woman's emotional and changeable lovemaking style. The secret of her desire begins long before she reaches the bedroom; the truth be told, she looks for "potential" in her mate—financially, socially, and sexually. She is also a communicator and an intellectual, so words and language are important to her. Poets and musicians can easily steal her heart.

Rat females need beauty around them to feel sexy. Fragrant candles, a bubble bath, and sensual music all expand her desire and prepare her mind and body to love you. She will be brought to ecstasy if you run your fingers with a feather light touch over her stomach and lower abdomen up to her breasts. Make small light circles around her nipples, drawing heat and energy there. Increase the pressure of the circles according to her level of arousal and gently roll her nipple between your index finger and thumb. You can switch to using your mouth there as well. There is a direct connection between her nipples and her genitals, so stimulating the nipples and areolae starts the Rat woman's fire in other areas.

Compatibilities

Romantically, the best match for the Rat is with Ox, Dragon, or Monkey souls. Pass on love relationships with the Goat and Horse.

Rat (+ yang):

Soul mate to—Ox

In trine with—Monkey, Dragon

In opposition to—Horse

Combatant to—Goat

In kind with—Ox

Resolving karma with—Rabbit

Steed—Tiger

Peach blossom—Rooster

Rat—Rat

These two like-minded souls will seek to achieve complete merging of body and soul. Both are imaginative lovers who refuse to settle down in routine. However, both being yang (+) souls, it is important for each to take the lead in romance. Each partner's high-strung disposition may exacerbate worries, affecting productivity.

Rat—Ox

The sentimental Rat is so vulnerable to her soul mate the Ox that this tender soul may sacrifice her finances on love's altar. There is nothing too good or too costly for her beloved Ox. With this potent combination, the Rat's usual perceptive discernment and shrewd financial sense can go right out the window.

Rat—Tiger

This unlikely match is a common one that "looks good on paper" but may fail to provide emotional satisfaction to both parties. The Tiger can overshadow his Rat partner just by being himself, and the fact that he is always on the go can leave his Rat partner feeling abandoned and inadequate.

Rat—Rabbit

A Rat soul cannot live without passion, so the detached Rabbit can leave the Rat feeling empty and abandoned. The Rabbit is not as invested in the relationship as his Rat partner, so he often ends up becoming the artful dodger.

Rat—Dragon

When these two are married, emotional security reins supreme—even in the face of a dalliance. If a choice must be made between a spouse and a lover, there is no contest. Both of these souls recognize and respect the other's taste for variety.

Rat—Snake

When it comes to lovemaking, the Rat is a master and virtuoso. Sex is something she is capable of surrendering herself to, body and soul. This proclivity interests the Snake, but the Snake's taste for forbidden fruit could devastate the hypersensitive Rat's sense of home and hearth. The Rat will rarely forgive an infidelity in this case.

Rat—Horse

Interestingly, despite their opposition, these two souls hook up with each other frequently. In Rats there exists a dichotomy—namely, their need for security versus their need for independence. They need an understanding ear to listen to their ideas, but Horses are too preoccupied with their own dreams and ambitions. This is a relationship that can end in bitterness.

Rat—Goat

This relationship is a comedy of errors. By the time the leisurely Goat wakes up to face the world, the energetic Rat has almost completed her day. In this pairing, hyperactivity meets sloth, and the results can be inharmonious to say the least.

Rat—Monkey

Sexuality is a fine art as well as a science between Rats and Monkeys. These two love each other and are not bashful about showing it. They may have many exhausting nights of love, intertwined with intellectual conversations and confidences.

Rat—Rooster

The Rat and the Rooster are in a "peach blossom" relationship, the kind responsible for torrid love affairs and emotional roller coaster rides. This is a love/hate relationship in which the Rat usually ends up with the short end of the stick. This is a difficult pairing of energies, as the peach blossom connection can easily become "forbidden fruit."

Rat—Dog

The Rat can't help correcting the Dog's all-too-human errors, which makes the Dog feel belittled and subpar—a disaster from the insecure Dog's point of view. The dynamic between these two resembles that of a parent/child relationship, one that leads to power struggles and difficult interactions. Any infidelity on the Rat's part will be considered absolute treason by the faithful Dog.

Rat—Pig

Rats have a tendency to feel as if nobody understands them. Feeling understood in a love relationship is important for the Rat's peace of mind, and the compassionate Pig fits the emotional bill nicely. (But then, who doesn't get along with the Pig?)

CHAPTER 18

鼠牛虎兔龍蛇馬羊猴鷄犬猪

ORAL OX

Feb 19, 1901 to Feb 7, 1902: Metal Ox
Feb 6, 1913 to Jan 25, 1914: Water Ox
Jan 25, 1925 to Feb 12, 1926: Wood Ox
Feb 11, 1937 to Jan 30, 1938: Fire Ox
Jan 29, 1949 to Feb 16, 1950: Earth Ox
Feb 15, 1961 to Feb 4, 1962: Metal Ox
Feb 3, 1973 to Jan 22, 1974: Water Ox
Feb 20, 1985 to Feb 8, 1986: Wood Ox
Feb 7, 1997 to Jan 27, 1998: Fire Ox
Jan 26, 2009 to Feb 13, 2010: Earth Ox

Needs: respect, security

Hates: noncompliance, insubordination

Turn-ons: nature, simplicity, sincerity

Turnoffs: condescension

Slow and sure, those born into Ox years are the marathon lovers of the Chinese Zodiac. Both male and female Oxen embody endurance—in and out of the bedroom—and possess a "lone wolf" style of romance. Home-spun Oxen is practical, earthy, and sensual, with a notable gift for manual dexterity and working with their hands. Not surprisingly, they are experts in the art of sensual stroking. Those born into Ox years need a down-to-earth partner of substance and loyalty. Their most amorous time is during the quiet, post-midnight hours between 1 a.m. and 3 a.m.

Oxen like to express their love in pragmatic ways rather than in trite romantic displays, and this can cause long-term partners to gradually become dispassionate or unromantic. Experimenting or trying something new in the bedroom is important for the Ox, who tends to play it safe sexually, and to whom romantic change doesn't come easy. Wild sexual ways aren't necessary to have a major effect on the Ox's love life—merely revisiting or reinventing some of the traditional romantic favorites can be a recipe for Ox paradise. A little change can have an exciting effect on the Ox's love life, so stoke up the fire and cuddle with your lover on a chilly winter evening, have a late dinner for two on the terrace, or just rediscover the simplicity of a bubble bath for two by candlelight.

If your man was born into an Ox year:

In romance, Oxen are vulnerable. They are patient and trusting of others, so their trust must be given to one who will never break their heart. Generally they are not men who take romantic risks, which means they often have to wait for romance. They are also patient and confident, however, so the wait for the woman of their dreams is no problem for them. Your Ox lover is a traditionalist and not one to wander far from home or chase wild erotic dreams. He is rational and emotionally stable, but never mistake this for shallow sentiments. The Ox man's sexuality runs deep and is as steady as a mountain. In bed, he is a slow starter, but will prove to be a sensual and long-lasting performer. He is also quite skilled with his hands. Once he has overcome his initial hesitation, your Ox man will show you just how skilled he really is when he plays you like a fine instrument.

Ox men search for a bit of an "old fashioned girl," one who is natural, sincere, and reverent of home, hearth, and family tradition. He is looking for you if you are the clean, scrubbed, girl-next-door type whom he can bring home to mom. In exchange for this honor he is prepared to show your own parents and family the utmost respect and attention. In marriage, Oxen are loyal, stable lovers, and they work hard at developing strong family bonds. In the Ox man's eyes, his partner, his family, and his offspring are sacred.

The Ox man loves life and *all* its carnal pleasures (he especially enjoys fine dining with good company and good wine), so love and sex occupy a large portion of his thoughts. He dreams of a Rubenesque, well-rounded goddess who is a tender earth mother and voluptuous lover combined in one earthbound angel. She should personify authority and compassion, strictness and good humor. His perfect woman will be found in blue jeans romping with a batch of puppies or kittens before she serves him up some of her homemade soup and biscuits. The woman of his dreams will then tuck their well scrubbed and happy cherubs into bed with a kiss and retire to her boudoir to prepare to love her man. Ah, can life get any better? Not if you're an Ox male.

Ox men strive to conceal their powerful sexuality beneath a casual front of ambition and material success. However, the hidden Element in the Ox year branch is Earth, and this shows up in his sex life. Partners can often be surprised and overwhelmed by the intense passion coming from beneath such a placid and cool exterior. Bubbling just below the surface is his sexual "magma," a passion that flows like lava from an erupting volcano. When aroused, Ox men are enthusiastic and confident in the art of love, but can be possessive or jealous if romantically threatened. If he is sure of his amorous ground, however, he will enjoy living up this "earthy" reputation.

In love and sex, the Ox male seeks duration in a relationship and stability in a partner. Not particularly interested in the modern or superficial, this stubborn, determined lover builds his love empire on solid rock. This is also a chivalrous man, one of times gone by who desires to protect his woman and who will rise to the occasion if needed. However, be forewarned that he is also extremely possessive and has a tendency to be jealous. Keep the talk about past boyfriends and partners to yourself, as you will be playing with fire if you ignite his primal territorial instincts.

If your woman was born into an Ox year:

The Ox woman is sensual but generally not romantic by modern standards. Love and sex are important to her, but partnership is of even higher priority. Stable and reliable similar to her Dog-year sisters, the Ox woman never approaches romance with a casual attitude. She seeks a down-to-earth partner of substance and loyalty, and once she finds her lover she is determined to keep him.

Maternal, sentimental, and slow to awake sexually, your Ox woman's bonds grow deeper with time. Fantasy and sexual imagination should be cultivated in the Ox-year woman, as her focus on the here-and-now and on routine can cause her libido to wane. Erogenous mental stimulation is very important to her. Classic erotic literature will fan her desire and indulge her love of history and days gone by.

The homespun Ox woman is practical and earthy, and like her Oxen brothers she is quite gifted with her hands. This is an area where the Ox woman really excels, and she is often an expert in the sensual art of penile stroking. Oils, lotions, and lubricants of all types can be found in her love chest, and are the first step to a memorable manual experience. After generously lubricating her man's penis as well as her hand, she begins slowly yet firmly stroking, keeping the pressure and speed constant and using smooth, fluid motions. Continued intense pressure will bring her man to orgasm, but since Taoist sexual practices separate orgasm and ejaculation, he may wish her to slow down so he can enjoy the ride in a more leisurely fashion. Between the testicles at the base of the penis is a very erotic spot that she can very gently touch or caress, along with the area of skin between his testicles and anus (the perineum).

The Ox woman is a sexually aware female, with a strong sensual appetite and a straightforward approach. Although she has the endurance to match the strongest male libido, her imagination is not always as active as it could be. She can easily get stuck in a romantic rut of repetitive routine. This is not a woman who will be found having sex on the sly in a public place or dressing up in a dominatrix costume. She prefers sex in the privacy of her bedroom and under more conventional circumstances. Having a dynamic sex life with an Ox woman may take some work. She needs to be vigilant in keeping the physical side of her love exciting. She shouldn't let self-consciousness keep her from trying new things, and she should never accept a so-so love life. If your love life with an Ox woman is fizzling, or if you and your partner have lapsed into lazy love habits, read Chapter 13 for some ideas to ignite passion.

Generally a late starter in sex, the Ox female has a natural self-sufficiency and sees many common romantic frills as silly. She considers love and sex an important but not dominant part of her life, so she doesn't put romance at the top of her priority list. Also, she is very strong-willed and may clash with her lover if he is equally strong-willed and tries to assert his authority over her. However, any man lucky enough to have her for a partner should consider himself truly blessed. She is sexually faithful and rarely will give her lover reason to be jealous. Ox women are also wonderful cooks, and if the old adage about the way to a man's heart being through his stomach is true, her beloved will seldom stray.

Compatibilities

Both the Rooster and the Snake are excellent choices for enduring relationships, but the soul mate for the Ox is the Rat. Partnerships with the Goat or the Horse may be particularly challenging.

Ox (- yin):

Soul mate to—Rat

In trine with—Snake, Rooster

In opposition to—Goat

Combatant to—Horse

In kind with—Rat

Resolving karma with—Dragon

Steed—Pig

Peach blossom—Horse

Ox—Rat

These two signs form a mutual admiration society and compliment each other well. Both souls are family- and security-oriented, and work well together in life and in love. When beside this soul mate the Ox remains devoted for life.

Ox—Ox

These two strong personalities can form a happy, quiet couple. It is important that both see eye-to-eye on key life issues such as religion and politics. Otherwise they may not be able to avoid a clash of wills. Both are placid, home-loving, and hardworking—characteristics that are often a recipe for success for this couple.

Ox—Tiger

Here we find "two cooks in the kitchen." These two natural leaders may vie for dominance in their relationship. Each party must have respect for their agreed-upon areas of authority.

Ox—Rabbit

These two are very "yin" and solitary loners by nature. No matter what the gender of each partner is, the Rabbit will expect the Ox to take the lead in this relationship. The Ox's brand of love is stable and practical while the Rabbit needs luxury and pampering.

Ox—Dragon

A clash of wills could derail the course of any long-term relationship between these two. Well-defined roles and mutual respect are critical in order for them to form a warm and enduring union.

Ox—Snake

These two karmic best friends enjoy a cozy, "fire-side" kind of relationship. Each has a deep understanding of the other. There is excellent compatibility in friendship and in marriage for these two like-minded souls.

Ox—Horse

The Horse would rather be any place except home. This is nothing less than treason to the Ox, who holds the family circle in such reverence. The Horse finds the Ox's stability boring, and neither sign has the foggiest idea of how the other thinks or feels.

Ox—Goat

This is a case of the motorcycle cop with the quota to meet versus the low-keyed, small-town sheriff who wants no confrontation. Oxen are regulated, organized, and controlled, while Goats are loose cannons who capriciously act and react to life. This is not an auspicious combination.

Ox—Monkey

Because of their self-sufficient and practical nature, love and sex are important but not absolutely essential to the Ox. This throws a wet blanket on the Monkey's enthusiasm, thereby creating a difficult relationship.

Ox—Rooster

The Ox delights in the company of the efficient Rooster. Whether it's a female Ox keeping the home fires burning for her Rooster military husband, or a male Ox enjoying watching his "little firecracker" of a wife efficiently run their home, this is a match made to last.

Ox—Dog

This pairing could be a maudlin pity party waiting to happen—the double dose of pessimism does neither of these two souls any good. However, the Dog has much compassion for the sweet-natured yet awkward Ox, so this can be a nurturing and loyal relationship.

Ox—Pig

These two calm souls speak the same language of quiet strength and old-fashioned virtues. However, the Ox and Pig do not normally gravitate to each other as they are both quiet and solitary souls. Unless they are introduced by a third party, their mutual reticence could prevent romantic sparks from igniting.

CHAPTER 19

鼠牛虎兔龍蛇馬羊猴鶏犬猪

TITILLATING TIGER

Feb 8, 1902 to Jan 28, 1903: Water Tiger
Jan 26, 1914 to Feb 13, 1915: Wood Tiger
Feb 13, 1926 to Feb 1, 1927: Fire Tiger
Jan 31, 1938 to Feb 18, 1939: Earth Tiger
Feb 17, 1950 to Feb 5, 1951: Metal Tiger
Feb 5, 1962 to Jan 24, 1963: Water Tiger
Jan 2, 31974 to Feb 10, 1975: Wood Tiger
Feb 9, 1986 to Jan 28, 1987: Fire Tiger
Jan 28, 1998 to Feb 15, 1999: Earth Tiger
Feb 14, 2010 to Feb 2, 2011: Metal Tiger
Needs: adventure, passion
Hates: routine, ingratitude
Turn-ons: full body massage
Turnoffs: boredom

Those born into Tiger years need to conquer sexually. The Tiger's need for passion and new triumphs can produce a tumultuous love life. Impetuous, independent, and impassioned, Tigers discover their sensuality early in life. Both male and female Tigers need to respect their lovers, and require a soul mate who is ready, eager, and willing to follow their lead. The hidden element in the Tiger branch is Wood, representing the upward and outward expansion of trees and vegetation. This is expressed in their sexuality as restlessness, territorial advance, and forward romantic momentum. Romantically intense and sexually possessive, Tigers thrive on risk and are known to seek out challenging lovers and partners.

When it comes to their need for independence, male and female Tigers show very little difference. Tigers value faithfulness, but should the whole affair move from commitment to confinement they are quite capable of moving on and starting anew. The strength, confidence, and passionate prowess that Tigers possess make them natural leaders in the dance of love. These mighty cats want to rule, but also to be admired; therefore they may test a lover from time to time just to reassure their desirability. This can create a love life filled with sexual tension. Even so, the Tiger's noble, generous, and giving nature makes certain that their lover will feel special.

If your man was born into a Tiger year:

The male Tiger exalts testosterone to new heights. His sexual virility as well as his personal magnetism is unsurpassed. This is a man who is fully capable of falling passionately in love and being completely carried away by his emotions. It's all or nothing with this ardent man—once he makes a love connection, he will devote himself body and soul. For the woman who wishes to be swept off her feet, the Tiger man will not disappoint. He likes a challenge, and women who are just a little out of reach fascinate him. Interesting, exotic, and even risky women hold a strong attraction for him. Mysterious and dangerous women turn him on. However, his possessiveness of his woman is as intense as his love of freedom. It is foolish to test this point with a Tiger.

Love is a most attractive state for the Tiger man, as pleasure, attraction, and the thrill of the chase are all states in which he thrives. As befits a natural leader, the Tiger man possesses great physical stamina, and marathon nights of lovemaking are his specialty. The 9 × 10 penile thrust sequence, in which he alternates between deep and shallow controlled thrusts, is also a favorite (for more on this technique, see Chapter 29). The Tiger man is a very confident lover who wants action first and foremost. He enjoys being admired (as he admires himself), so a few well-placed mirrors in the bedroom will stir his romantic embers.

He is also willing to take chances and gamble where romance and love are concerned. The word "losing" is not in his vocabulary. In love and sex, the Tiger male believes in seizing the moment; once you have aroused his interest, passionate fireworks will fly. This is a lover who knows how to turn up the heat.

If your woman was born into a Tiger year:

It is said that it can be lonely at the top, and in the realm of the heart, the capable Tigress knows this all too well. Her inner strength and profound independence can cause her difficulties when it comes to love and sex. Being so competent, she is not the type of woman men feel the need to rescue. She tends to come on too strong and frighten would-be lovers away. In addition, she can hold a fascination for weak or fainthearted men who are looking to be taken care of. Your average Tigress could never respect such a man and will quickly become domineering, overbearing, and romantically miserable. Coupled life with the female Tigress is not easy even under ideal circumstances, but if she does not admire her partner completely it can become a battlefield. This proud and assertive woman needs a strong, secure, and direct man whom she respects unconditionally, and a lover who is not threatened by her bravada, as she should never have to pretend to be less than she is. The rare man who tames this dynamic woman will be richly rewarded.

There are actually very few differences between the sexual psychology of male and female Tigers. However, the Tiger female is a feminist to her very core, and she often resents the power that her masculine counterparts wield. If there is a chink in the sexist male armor, this is the woman who will find it. As compared to other signs, a higher percentage of Tigresses choose other females as sexual partners. In love, her sincerity is rarely in question; rather, it is her unconventional methods that can raise some eyebrows. Supremely stubborn, she absolutely must be the captain of her own ship in every way, shape, and form.

When she decides to love and give her heart full rein, she loves with her whole being and expects the same from her partner. Complacency and routine are the death-blows to her passion. Despite her own passionate personality, however, she may have trouble abandoning herself to ecstasy. This is due to her pride, her outward toughness, and her unconscious unwillingness to submit to feminine stereotypes.

The female Tigress differs most notably from other women in her ability to make a clear distinction between love and sex. Just because she shared a night of passionate sex doesn't mean she expects (or will even accept) a ring on her finger or a commitment from her partner. Sexually, she expresses her wants and needs in a direct and forthright manner, is active in bed, and is at home taking the lead. The adventurous man who succeeds in capturing the Tigress's heart will need a strong libido, some impressive talents, and good character credentials. If this sounds like the woman for you, step right up—she's taking applications as we speak.

Compatibilities

Romantically, the best match for the Tiger is with the Horse and the Dog. Their soul mate is the honest and obliging Pig. Be cautious in love relationships with the Monkey, Snake, and other Tigers.

Tiger (+ yang):

Soul mate to—Pig

In trine with—Horse, Dog

In opposition to—Monkey

Combatant to—Snake

In kind with—Rabbit

Resolving karma with—Snake

Steed—Monkey

Peach blossom—Rabbit

Tiger—Rat

This union is a frustrating one for the couple. The Tiger is forthright and "transparent"—one always knows where they stand with him. In contrast, the Rat is inscrutable and mysterious. This is a relationship without any real connection, and each may eventually live a separate life.

Tiger—Ox

Here we find a karmic power struggle. More often than not, the Tiger's outgoing personality leaves the Ox in the shadows. This can easily embitter the Ox, who tires of the Tiger's perpetual place in the spotlight.

Tiger—Tiger

This combination is similar to two captains at the wheel, while the crew watches the two of them exhaust themselves as they vie for the top position. Many of the signs can cohabit peacefully with those of their own sign, but two Tigers are an exception.

Tiger—Rabbit

The Tiger's energy level and verve tends to overwhelm the easily beleaguered Rabbit. The Tiger is boisterous and fearless, while the Rabbit is understated and fainthearted. There are much better matches for both.

Tiger—Dragon

This is a sturdy relationship that can stand the test of time. These two sources of power are capable of formulating visionary plans of action and completing vast projects together. Above all, the Tiger and the Dragon are good friends.

Tiger—Snake

The action-oriented Tiger tends to be annoyed by the Snake's slow deliberations in life. Tigers move fast, think fast, and intend to cross life's finish line first. The Snake takes their time in everything they do, which the Tiger may perceive as laziness.

Tiger—Horse

These two kindred souls are natural friends and lovers. Like-minded in their pursuit of new challenges, the Tiger and Horse speak the same language of action, idealism, and improving the human condition.

Tiger—Goat

To be perfectly blunt, this is a terrible match. The Tiger is strong and independent and the Goat is weak and very dependent. The Goat's lack of ambition and slothful ways infuriate most Tigers.

Tiger—Monkey

There can be a trust issue between these two polarized souls. The Tiger has no patience for the Monkey's foolish schemes and tricks. This pairing makes better friends than lovers.

Tiger—Rooster

These two souls can have problems communicating. More than likely, this is an infatuation rather than a long-term union. The Tiger and the Rooster are "firecracker" personalities, so their union can spark some memorable verbal battles.

Tiger—Dog

If ever there were a karmic love affair, it would be between these two souls. The Tiger and the Dog are naturally drawn toward one another and interact with encouragement and generosity. The Tiger is the emperor and the Dog, their prime minister.

Tiger—Pig

While the Tiger is supremely compatible with both the Horse and the Dog, it is the honest and affectionate Pig who is the Tiger's soul mate. The sanguine Pig truly appreciates the Tiger's sublime qualities, and is never threatened by their grand accomplishments. In friendship and in love, this relationship is a keeper.

CHAPTER 20

鼠牛虎兔龍蛇馬羊猴鷄犬猪

RECEPTIVE RABBIT

Feb 14, 1915 to Feb 2, 1916: Wood Rabbit
Jan 29, 1903 to Feb 15, 1904: Water Rabbit
Feb 2, 1927 to Jan 22, 1928: Fire Rabbit
Feb 19, 1939 to Feb 7, 1940: Earth Rabbit
Feb 6, 1951 to Jan 26, 1952: Metal Rabbit
Jan 25, 1963 to Feb 12, 1964: Water Rabbit
Feb 11, 1975 to Jan 30, 1976: Wood Rabbit
Jan 29, 1987 to Feb 16, 1988: Fire Rabbit
Feb 16, 1999 to Feb 4, 2000: Earth Rabbit
Feb 3, 2011 to Jan 22, 2012: Metal Rabbit
Needs: serenity, privacy
Hates: unpleasantness, entrapment
Turn-ons: romantic dinners, slow seduction
Turnoffs: loud, crass people

Refinement and subtlety are at the top of the receptive Rabbit's arsenal of aphrodisiacs. Street-wise, charming, and very, very smooth, Rabbits are creative, albeit aloof lovers. Gentle and somewhat passive, Rabbits enjoy being sexually pampered, coddled, and indulged by their lovers. The Rabbit is one of the most sexual of the signs, but they are not known to have sexual relationships of long duration; they are spiritually wired for short-term affairs rather than long-term commitments. They find it even more difficult to actually fall in love. This is due to a love of virtue and a desire for perfection in their partner. Very refined and introverted, Rabbits are sexually reserved and often on guard. Both males and females are uncomfortable displaying their romantic feelings, and consider public displays and emotional outbursts rather ridiculous.

It is characteristic of Rabbits to be attracted to both older and younger lovers, and also to unavailable or unattainable partners. Keeping the course of love a bit off-balance allows the Rabbit to keep their options open, thus maintaining their psychological independence. There exists a higher percentage of bachelors and bachelorettes amongst those born into Rabbit years than in any other sign. But it is also true that, once committed, Rabbits are affectionate, devoted, and supportive partners. The favored time of day for Rabbits to make love is during the early morning dawn hours between 5 a.m. and 7 a.m.

If your man was born into a Rabbit year:

The Rabbit's essence of detachment shows up in his quiet and cool "yin" sexuality. This isn't a man given to displays of passion or chivalry, so if his lover wants him to, say, slay a dragon for her, she may be waiting for quite a while. He is generally passive when making love, and may appear lost inside his own head somewhere. He tends to have sex next to his partner rather than with her. The Rabbit man also likes sexual variety and may have difficulty maintaining a monogamous relationship for an extended period of time. However, if a sensitive, imaginative, and slow-handed lover is on your wish list, the Rabbit man will be a perfect fit.

The Rabbit man's creative mind is fertile ground for fantasy. This can be good or bad, depending on his focus. On the positive side, he knows how to be a good friend and how to listen to his lover. He is a well-mannered gentleman who is fun to be with, easygoing, and highly creative sexually. He is also a private man who keeps his own council, but can always be counted on for good advice. However, because of his sharp sense of observation, he tends to be quietly critical of his woman's physical appearance; for this reason his partner needs to be immaculately groomed and well-put-together at all times. He prefers smaller, thinner, more androgynous women. He won't tell you so necessarily (as he generally has very good manners), but packing on the pounds will affect his passion toward you.

Many a lusty wench well-qualified to keep her Rabbit man purring has tried to coax, convince, and otherwise sexually entice him into a life as a couple, to no avail. The Rabbit male needs, seeks out, and will not settle for anything less than an independent partner who makes very few demands on his time and privacy. Basically, this feature is at the root of a Rabbit man's commitment phobia. He fears losing the ability to escape everyone and everything if he needs to. Plus, forever is a long time to his way of thinking. But he's torn: He needs love and affection as much as the next person, and will expect his lover to be available for him, to pleasure and to comfort him—until he decides it's time for some "personal space." Don Quixote, Rudolph Valentino, and the artful dodger all rolled into one— that's your Rabbit man. If his partner is not available when he desires her, there is the likelihood that he will wander in search of another, more attentive lover's nest. The lyricist who wrote the words, "If you can't be with the one you love, love the one you're with," was most assuredly a Rabbit male.

Despite all this, the Rabbit male is a master of sensual subtlety. He has a profound liking for secrecy, and sexual secrets are his specialty: He will want you to tell him yours, and in return he will share a few of his own with you as well. For the woman who wishes to discover the secret treasures of sensuality that her Rabbit man is capable of, she must look beyond his appearance. Smart women turn him on. Intellectuals, professionals, and other high achievers have the advantage with him. The Rabbit man prefers either authoritarian and powerful women or just the opposite— humble, younger girls of unfortunate or poverty-stricken circumstances. He can see the diamond in the rough, and with his help his tattered maid becomes Cinderella.

Be forewarned, however, that the timorous Rabbit male is distrustful, suspicious, and petrified of entrapment. They mistrust emotions of all kinds, particularly their own. No matter how beautiful or charming the woman, the Rabbit man is not easily seduced. Although he enjoys a healthy sexual appetite, his heart is terminally under the influence of his mind; for this reason your Rabbit man can appear aloof or indifferent sexually. He may also suffer from phobias or inhibitions and may need you to help boost his self-confidence. In addition, he possesses an overdeveloped sense of virtue, decency, and unbalanced perfectionism. Because of this he can be on a romantic quest for the "perfect" woman—an ideal combination of all women, an angel.

The Rabbit man's sexual desire waxes and wanes according to the state of his nerves and emotions at any given time. He needs a harmonious atmosphere conducive to relaxation in order to be able to perform well sexually. When he's stressed or extremely tired, his woman must take the lead. The female superior position is a great choice in this instance, as he can relax his jostled nerves for a while and just enjoy. This also puts him in a position to caress his lover's breasts while she works him up to a fever pitch by stimulating her own clitoris and bringing herself to orgasm as he watches from below.

The Rabbit male does make an adorable lover, and if he so chooses he knows how to show great understanding and tenderness to his beloved. However, his concern and love can vanish as fast as a vapor if cheated or crossed. Under the right circumstances, he can be vindictive and have a heart as cold as stone.

If your woman was born into a Rabbit year:

The Rabbit woman dreams of the man who knows how to unite strength with tenderness, whether he is a professional, an intellectual, or a construction worker. Reflective of the negative, feminine night force, her sexuality is receptive and deep. From a young age, this angel of femininity has nurtured the ability to charm the opposite sex. Refinement, decorum, and delicacy are her main weapons of love, and when it comes to men she is a woman of good taste. This delicate and tactful lady keeps a tight reign over her emotions and is not prone to being overly emotional or overly affectionate. She may adore her man, but unbridled passion and overt displays of affection make her uncomfortable. However, she makes a sweet, attentive, and tasteful lover, as well as an intelligent companion and confidant whose advice is invaluable.

Tactful and considerate, she knows how to please and pleasure her man and does so in a sedate and calm manner. Her sexual style is cool, detached, and knowing. She will always keep her distance, but part of her unique charm is her reticence. She fans her lover's fire by making him feel as if her love is still to be won. With her aura of sexual purity, delicacy, and reserve, the Rabbit woman needs a wise and skilled lover who will be able to release her passion and sexual abandon. It is a rare man who possesses the key to unlocking her fervor in the bedroom, but he will be well rewarded. Ultimately, she can only give herself sexually to a man who has won her respect.

Her lover can break through her inhibitions and show his good taste by using the "black pearl" technique. In this, he places a small pillow under her buttocks, raising her pelvis just slightly, as she lies on her back and he kneels or lies prone between her legs. He takes her clitoris gently in his mouth and sucks, moving up and down her clitoral shaft using the same rhythmic motions he himself would like used on his penis during fellatio. Simultaneously, he inserts his finger about two finger widths deep into her vagina and curls his finger upward toward the front (anterior) vaginal wall in order to stimulate her G-spot. This combination is absolutely mind-boggling for the woman, and it's a major turn-on for her lover to see her abandon herself to such pleasure!

A beautiful atmosphere alive with delicious scents, candles, and sensual music is a must for the Rabbit female. Her boudoir will be a beautiful and harmonious haven, strewn with silk and velvet pillows and inviting ambiance. She needs to be romanced and enticed into relaxing enough to enjoy the physical side of love. The man who wins her heart and gains the privilege of sharing her pillow can expect a faithful, homespun, and discreet companion. Her lover must always handle her with care and gentility—or, as a wise Taoist once said, "Stimulate the lotus but do not harm the petals."

Compatibilities

Sexually, the best match for the Rabbit is with the Goat or Pig; however their soul mate is found with the devoted Dog. Be cautious in sexual and love relationships with the Dragon and Rooster.

Rabbit (- yin):

Soul mate to—Dog

In trine with—Goat, Pig

In opposition to—Rooster

Combatant to—Dragon

In kind with—Tiger

Resolving karma with—Horse

Steed—Snake

Peach blossom—Rat

Rabbit—Rat

The Rabbit is not as invested in the relationship as his Rat partner is and thus can become emotionally unavailable. Both share a love of the fine arts and scholarly pursuits, but this pairing makes better friends than lovers.

Rabbit—Ox

These two are solitary loners by nature. The Rabbit can suffer from a lack of romance with the Ox. The Ox's brand of love is stable and practical, but the Rabbit needs luxury, romance, and pampering.

Rabbit—Tiger

The Rabbit can be overwhelmed by the Tiger's brusque ways. The Rabbit is a good friend and adviser to the Tiger, but there are better matches for each of these two.

Rabbit—Rabbit

Two Rabbits in tandem would be a veritable whirlwind tour of museums, concerts, and art galleries. This is a gentle combination of kindred spirits, and an auspicious partnership in both friendship and love. Together they create an eternal party and enjoy many a fireside chat.

Rabbit—Dragon

Unfortunately, the Rabbit and the Dragon are only one sign (and many times only one year) apart, and thus are often thrown together as classmates, colleagues, and spouses. The Rabbit is refined and mannerly while the Dragon is crass and outspoken, which creates many tensions.

Rabbit—Snake

The Rabbit and the Snake are polished, creative, and philosophical souls who enjoy one another's company. However, despite sharing a taste for the finer things in life, they will experience a difficult union. The Snake has the potential to consume the Rabbit.

Rabbit—Horse

These two always have an enjoyable time together, and the Rabbit doesn't mind staying home and enjoying their privacy while the Horse conquers new pastures. This pairing works as a good friendship and is a workable union.

Rabbit—Goat

These two are best friends and speak a similar language of propriety and creativity. They walk hand-in-hand on the road toward ultimate enlightenment. In their quest to find and create beauty in this life, the Rabbit and the Goat form a melodious union.

Rabbit—Monkey

The Rabbit finds the Monkey a little too superficial for her taste. The Monkey can't resist tricking the Rabbit, but the Rabbit is prepared with some tricks of her own. This is not a beneficial relationship for either sign.

Rabbit—Rooster

No matter how hard these two try, compatibility seems beyond their reach. The brash Rooster's caustic criticism sets the delicate Rabbit's nerves on edge. While relationships between all signs are possible, this combination of souls is almost always a recipe for disaster.

Rabbit—Dog

These two souls recognize each other immediately, as most have karmic links from other times and places. If the "attached" Dog and the "detached" Rabbit can overcome their fears and their trust issues, this is a match made in heaven.

Rabbit—Pig

This is a sweet relationship between two gentle souls. Both are well-mannered and genuinely virtuous. The diplomatic and socially adept Rabbit aids and befriends the shy Pig, to the benefit of both. These two are unmistakably good partners.

CHAPTER 21

鼠牛虎兔龍蛇馬羊猴雞犬猪

DRAGON DEBAUCHERY

Feb 16, 1904 to Feb 3, 1905: Wood Dragon
Feb 3, 1916 to Jan 22, 1917: Fire Dragon
Jan 23, 1928 to Feb 9, 1929: Earth Dragon
Feb 8, 1940 to Jan 26, 1941: Metal Dragon
Jan 27, 1952 to Feb 13, 1953: Water Dragon
Feb 13, 1964 to Feb 1, 1965: Wood Dragon
Jan 31, 1976 to Feb 17, 1977: Fire Dragon
Feb 17, 1988 to Feb 5, 1989: Earth Dragon
Feb 5, 2000 to Jan 23, 2001: Metal Dragon
Jan 23, 2012 to Feb 9, 2013: Water Dragon
Needs: admiration
Hates: small cramped spaces
Turn-ons: thunderstorms, movies, the theatre
Turnoffs: weakness

The powerful Dragon is the physically healthy, utopian visionary of the Chinese Zodiac. A lucky star shines on those souls born into Dragon years, especially in matters of the heart. Outspoken, animated, and ardent for love, Dragons possess boundless sexual energy and vital ching qi (sexual energy.) Imaginative and very "yang" lovers, these proud souls do not like to be challenged, in life or in the bedroom. Their essential nature of "unpredictability" keeps love fresh, albeit filled with drama at times.

Egotistic and always high profile, Dragons are assertive, extroverted, and downright boisterous lovers. Successful and socially popular, Dragons were born to be in the public eye, and they enjoy having an attractive partner on their arm. Their sexual selection process is guided by a deep need to be respected and admired. Demanding, original, and enthusiastic, the hot-blooded Dragon needs an acquiescing or submissive love partner.

Possessing a taste for the unusual, the bizarre, and the sexually diverse, Dragons can be infatuate and savor many love partners throughout their lives. In love, they are autonomous souls and will never put their life on hold for romance. Seldom in a hurry to surrender their freedom to marriage, Dragons enjoy legions of admirers, but may choose to remain single or marry later in life. When they do marry, their existence is independent from their choice of marriage partner.

Dragon souls gather sexual qi during the mid-morning hours between 7 a.m. and 9 a.m.

If your man was born into a Dragon year:

The bedroom—and indeed the world in general—is the Dragon male's stage. Drama, excitement, and extravagance are the critical components in his sexual psychology. This is an overwhelming yang lover who stoops to conquer his woman. Similar to his Rabbit brothers, the Dragon man has some very high standards for the woman of his fantasies. Because he looks for perfection in a partner, and because he is sexually wired for short-term affairs rather than long-term relationships, he can have trouble maintaining a monogamous relationship of long duration. This same perfectionism makes it even more difficult for him to fall deeply in love. For this reason, his love life may resemble a roller coaster of ups and downs, and feature a romantic resume of love affairs that begin quickly and end abruptly. Luckily for him, the Dragon man can easily forget his sorrows and quickly resume his romantic quest. This instability in matters of the heart is particularly problematic during early adulthood, but tends to ease up as middle age approaches (the "Metal Element" period between the ages of 36 and 48).

While the Dragon man's monogamy may be uncertain, his powerful sex drive is not. He is a marathon lover who possesses great passion and stamina. He is also sentimental, ardent, and capable of sweeping a woman off her feet. When he loves, he loves with the style of a grand showman and engages his partner totally. He likes to amaze the object of his affections and protect her with his theatrical demonstrations of chivalry. It is important to your Dragon man that he appear strong and romantically in control. This isn't a male who enjoys being babied or coddled, as he feels this may make him look weak in your eyes. And "weak" is a four letter word to this gentleman. The Dragon male wants to be his lover's caretaker and have her rely on him and need what he has to offer. This confirms to him his power and importance in her life.

The vain and egotistical Dragon male is susceptible to compliments and even flattery, but he will not tolerate competition from other men under any circumstances or in any form. If his pride is wounded, his ego bruised, or if he's feeling powerless, he can indeed breathe fire and be a very difficult beast to live with. Despite his exceedingly high opinion of himself, the male Dragon truly intends to be an excellent partner, lover, and husband. However, there is a price to be paid for admission to his love lair: His partner must put her personal ambitions second to his. He will expect her to devote herself body and soul to his success and live as second in command.

He has a thirst for physical beauty and glamorous women—a thirst equal only to his hunger for admiration. The woman of his dreams must be an exquisite creature, an ideal combination of all women, really. Most importantly, she must be an angel in the living room yet a devil in the bedroom. He looks for aesthetic qualities in a woman, and wants their lovemaking to be "picture perfect." And speaking of photogenic—being the consummate showman, your Dragon relishes the thought of himself in the role of erotic director, and may wish to videotape the two of you making love. He may also have a strong attraction to voyeurism and group sex. Additionally, direct and intense eye contact during sex is important to him, so the face-to-face "soulmating" position is a favorite.

Essentially, this is a man who needs his lover to be submissive and subservient to him. Not in a mean or tyrannical way—he simply has to be the one who calls the romantic shots. A crass or careless woman can injure his brittle self-image and be a death-blow to his libido. If she wounds him deeply enough, he will search for comfort and fulfill his ego requirements in the arms of another woman. He may even become temporarily impotent. Although he can be a good spouse and lover, he is a demanding partner who wants his woman to follow his lead, even if that means blindly following him where angels dare not tread.

If your woman was born into a Dragon year:

The Dragon woman seldom allows love to become the highest priority in her life. She wants love and companionship as much as the next woman, but she is not prepared to sacrifice the other aspects of her life for it. Romance is just a small part of her quest for admiration in this life. She sees herself mirrored in her lover's eyes and wants this to be a flattering portrait. Simply put, she likes men who like her. If he is enamored with her, she reasons, he *must* have good taste.

Personable and beautiful, Dragon women seldom have a shortage of admirers who are ready and willing to follow her wherever she may go. However, selecting just one man to the exclusion of all the rest doesn't sit well with her. She would prefer to be perpetually and eternally romanced by a variety of men. This goddess of love is forever searching for her next Adonis, and on this she is not willing to compromise.

Her choice in men is influenced by her subconscious need to be praised and admired. Akin to her Dog-year sisters, she can take on difficult partners, convinced of the power of her brand of love to save and rehabilitate them. If there is some publicity or recognition from others involved in this salvation, so much the better. She is more than capable of true and profound romantic love if she is aware of the cosmic influences, and recognizes her true love when he crosses her path.

When she is with a lover whom she respects unconditionally (and vice versa), the female Dragon proves to be an extraordinary and exciting partner. When a relationship is severed, the Dragon woman is resilient—generally it is her partner who will be the most devastated. If she becomes a victim of bad romantic luck, the Dragon female (as with her Tiger sisters) may balk at social customs and chose lesbianism as an alternative life style. She will usually prefer a more dominant role in such relationships. No matter what lifestyle she chooses, this powerful and outspoken woman must never be taken for granted; otherwise she may retaliate in her own way. She may either just turn off sexually or seek intimacy with another partner. Her sexual expression needs a dramatic avenue, even if that involves provoking an argument simply for the pleasure of making up later!

Because she has a preference for taking the lead in the bedroom, she will enjoy the "little stream" position. In this, she has her lover lie on his back with his legs together and extended out straight. She sits atop his forelegs facing him, and bends her legs and extends them along side of his as she rests her weight on her knees and legs. She moves her buttocks forward, gradually allowing only the head of his penis to penetrate her. The trick of this technique is to allow only shallow penetrations, which she can control in any way she desires. This teases her man's "jade stem" and brings him to a powerful orgasm.

The Dragon female has an exceptional capacity for love, both emotionally and physically. There are many erotic delights in store for the lover who is willing to admire and even worship this combination of Aphrodite and Venus wrapped up into one femme fatal.

Compatibilities

Romantically, the best match for the Dragon is with those born during Rat or Monkey years; however, their true soul mate is found with the candid Rooster. Be cautious in love relationships with the Dog and Rabbit.

Dragon (+ yang):

Soul mate to—Rooster

In trine with—Rat, Monkey

In opposition to—Dog

Combatant to—Rabbit

In kind with—Snake

Resolving karma with—Goat

Steed—Tiger

Peach blossom—Rooster

Dragon—Rat

Both of these souls recognize each other's taste for variety. When married, the Dragon and Rat work as a team, and emotional security reins supreme. They both share a love of socializing, but the Rat will never upstage their cherished Dragon.

Dragon—Ox

A clash of wills prevents any long-term relationship between these two. Both the Dragon and Ox need admiration, and it is not forthcoming from either. Well-defined roles and mutual respect are critical for any relationship between them.

Dragon—Tiger

This pairing creates a sturdy though high-drama relationship. Both are powerful and willful souls who are able to work together, play together, and love together.

Dragon—Rabbit

The Dragon bowls the Rabbit over with their force of will and over-bearing conduct. The Dragon's direct and blunt manner can embarrass the courteous and gracious Rabbit.

Dragon—Dragon

This "priest" and "priestess" couple of the Chinese Zodiac is an amazing pair. This union has the potential for extremes, both good and bad. For this relationship to work, they must hold each other in the highest esteem, and both must have their own stage on which to shine.

Dragon—Snake

This is a relationship that has the potential for happiness if the possessive Snake will allow the autonomous Dragon to leave the lair from time to time. Infidelity could become an issue with this couple, but if the union is severed they will continue to remain friends.

Dragon—Horse

There is a profound clash of egos between the self-assured Dragon and the self-absorbed Horse. Both prefer to be center stage and neither is prepared to bow to the other. This is a superficial relationship at best.

Dragon—Goat

This unlikely pairing can work wonderfully if the Dragon is male and the Goat is female. The Dragon must use delicacy and gentleness to keep from overwhelming the Goat. This is a potentially strong and lasting attraction.

Dragon—Monkey

These two compatible souls seek each other out and speak a similar language of unpredictability, irrepressibility, and innovation. The Dragon and Monkey have an excellent chance for a stimulating and enduring relationship.

Dragon—Rooster

These two soul mates are a match made in heaven. The Rooster has the pluck and audacity to hold the interest of the bold Dragon. Together they make a handsome and lively couple.

Dragon—Dog

This is an interesting relationship to say the least. Being polarized opposites, the Dragon and the Dog are as different as night and day. However, each possesses traits that the other would do well to learn. They make better colleagues than lovers.

Dragon—Pig

Almost everyone gets along well with the sweet-natured Pig, and the Dragon is no exception. A wide and smooth path to romance awaits these two.

CHAPTER 22

鼠牛虎兔龍蛇馬羊猴鷄犬猪

SEXY SNAKE

Feb 4, 1905 to Jan 24, 1906: Wood Snake
Jan 23, 1917 to Feb 10, 1918: Fire Snake
Feb 10, 1929 to Jan 29, 1930: Earth Snake
Jan 27, 1941 to Feb 14, 1942: Metal Snake
Feb 14, 1953 to Feb 2, 1954: Water Snake
Feb 2, 1965 to Jan 20, 1966: Wood Snake
Feb 18, 1977 to Feb 6, 1978: Fire Snake
Feb 6, 1989 to Jan 26, 1990: Earth Snake
Jan 24, 2001 to Feb 11, 2002: Metal Snake
Feb 10, 2013 to Jan 30, 2014: Water Snake
Needs: privacy
Hates: crass, boorish people
Turn-ons: music, secrets
Turnoffs: vulgarity

The Snake is the wise philosopher and sensualist of the Chinese Zodiac. Both male and female Snakes enjoy the spiritual side of sex and naturally gravitate toward tantric and Taoist practices. Seduction, secrets, and savvy are the sexy Snake's charms. This highly erogenous sign seeks an ardent partner who surrenders to passion and responds to slow seduction.

Physically attractive and blessed with satin skin, many seductresses and master lovers were born into Snake years. Snakes project a quiet, accumulated energy and are turned on by the deep and aesthetic sides of love and sex. Unusually perceptive and multi-sensory, Snakes are sensual and intuitive lovers.

Their method of seduction is an arousing mixture of attractiveness, sensuality, and enhanced intuition. Along with their magical charm and irresistible sexuality, Snakes of both sexes can also offer fascinating insights and impeccable advice. In love, Snakes are jealous and possessive, and crave sleepless nights of passionate lovemaking and intimate secrets. This is a lover who desires to be totally merged with their partner and know even the most intimate details of their soul.

Immersed and enmeshed on a deep level when in love, Snakes intuitively kindle, feed, and fan love's fire. They choose their partners cautiously, allowing a relationship to slowly accumulate energy as they examine it for potential longevity. Snakes gather sexual stamina during the late morning hours between 9 a.m. and 11 a.m.

If your man was born into a Snake year:

Snake men are extraordinarily handsome and have a notorious reputation for being consummate Casanovas and passionate playboys. Feelings, eroticism, and subtlety are embedded in his sexual psychology. Seduction is the name of his game, and he gives new meaning to the words "smooth moves." Although he is oozing with pheromones and ardent desire, this man seldom rushes in to the act of love. He waits, allowing his passion to percolate until the timing is just right.

The woman of his dreams is a refined princess who is slightly indifferent to his charms—one who will make him burn to possess her. Few things ignite his flames like a cool, nonchalant woman who plays slightly hard to get and proves difficult for him to conquer. The woman who will capture his heart (and body) is exquisitely beautiful, slightly fragile, and extraordinarily feminine. Women who are physically and emotionally healthy turn him on, as do glamorous and sophisticated femmes adorned in luxury and elegance. Models, debutantes, and chic women have a definite advantage with him as well.

A die-hard romantic, your Snake man is in love with love itself! To him, life is meaningless if he doesn't have the fairer sex to walk hand-in-hand with. Whether he is an incorrigible sheik in the desert of love or a refined ladies' man of finesse and charm, the Snake man has an irresistible charm for virtually all women. His extreme popularity with the ladies is due to his multifaceted balance of spiritual, mental, and physical energies. He will be his lover's spiritual adviser, psychiatrist, and sensual lover all in one.

Pursuing the fairer sex is a passion and a popular pastime for the Snake man. This talent can come back to haunt him if he finds he has fallen in love with two women at once. He is no stranger to the love triangle, and he seems to find himself frequently caught in a tangled web of his own spinning. However, he wants everyone to be happy, and he prides himself on being especially cautious with women's feelings.

The woman who loves him must never upset his sense of serenity or topple his delicate emotional tower. He will also need special indulgence with his peculiar food likes and dislikes, eccentric personal habits, and his procrastinating ways. However, his woman's biggest hurdle by far will be his flirtatious behavior and fascination with sexual variety. The Snake man will seldom hide his fixations or adventures, as he sees nothing wrong with his intentions or dalliances.

This is an experienced lover whose sexual magnetism is exceptionally strong, and who knows his way around a woman's body as if it were his own. There truly is no more skilled and intuitive lover than the Snake man. He "uses the force" when making love, and sensual intuition flows from every pore of his being. He inherently understands the concept of yin/yang exchange in sexuality, and sees intercourse as a means for his body, mind, and spirit to dance. A master in the art of orally pleasuring a woman, the Snake male also wrote the book on "tongue kung fu." He knows this is the quickest way to bring his lover to a rapid boil and for her to become fully lubricated for the pleasures to come. His lips and tongue are much more suitable for stimulating the delicate clitoris than his fingers. Taoist tongue strengthening exercises—in which he sticks out his tongue as far as possible (as is natural for the Snake) and then retracts it back into his mouth—can help him cultivate his technique. He can then start at her vaginal opening and lick his way up to her clitoris, rolling his tongue gently in small circular motions and flicking the tip of it every few rotations. If he inserts his finger into her vagina and simultaneously stimulates her G-spot, he can bring his lover to orgasmic euphoria.

If your woman was born into a Snake year:

It is said that it is most fortunate for a family to be blessed with a daughter born into a year of the Snake, as she will be both wise and beautiful. The Snake woman is a romantic who firmly believes in the kind of enchantment found in fairy tales. Desire makes its way into every nook of the Snake woman's life. For her, the preliminaries of love are as important as the sexual act itself. Seduction, knowing looks, and subtlety turn her on, and refined and powerful men who prove difficult to charm entice her. Spontaneity guides her passion; however, because she is of the feminine, yin night-force, she is willing to take a passive role, and will be completely happy allowing her mate to dominate her.

The Snake woman moves within her own subtle and balanced universe of charm and beauty. Coarse, crude, earthbound, petty, inconsiderate, or brutal men are surefire turnoffs for her. Instead, she seeks out a sensitive, soft-spoken gentleman of good taste and culture. "007" spy types, and stealthy, wealthy, and wise men of sophistication who travel the world, race sport boats, or write great novels capture her heart. Additionally, she loves to be pampered with luxury and the finer things in life, so the lover who enjoys her favors will want to have a healthy bank account.

She sincerely likes men, and her social advancement, material security, and comfort are closely tied to her choice of partner. Coy, capricious, and slightly mysterious, she may ask her man to slay a dragon for her (if she deems it necessary), as she is a woman who needs frequent reassurance of her lover's devotion. Her lover should never take her for granted, as she isn't naturally monogamous and won't lose sleep over any infidelities she may commit. However, she will be jealous and possessive of her beloved. Indeed, hell hath no fury like a rejected Snake female. She is capable of carrying grudges of long duration, and if the wound is grievous enough, she will serve her revenge cold.

Compatibilities

Romantically, the best match for the Snake is with those born during Ox or Rooster years; however their soul mate is found with the mercurial Monkey. Be cautious in love relationships with the Tiger and Pig.

Snake (- yin):

Soul mate to—Monkey

In trine with—Ox, Rooster

In opposition with—Pig

Combatant to—Tiger

In kind with—Dragon

Resolving karma with—Monkey

Steed—Pig
Peach blossom—Horse

Snake—Rat

The Rat is a sensual master, and sex is something he is capable of surrendering to completely. However, the Snake has the ability to devour the Rat, body and soul. The Rat may suffer heartache in this relationship.

Snake—Ox

These two best friends have a deep understanding of each other. This pairing has excellent compatibility in both friendship and marriage. These two like-minded souls can form a union of long duration.

Snake—Tiger

The Snake's slow calculating and endless pondering about the meaning of life annoys and frustrates the Tiger. In this relationship, the Snake may constantly feel pushed and prodded out of her comfort zone and into a more stressed and harried lifestyle. The Snake should look for a less impulsive partner.

Snake—Rabbit

As they both share a taste for luxury and the finer things in life, the Snake and Rabbit could very well find themselves together. However, the Snake is always in charge of the relationship's direction, and may or may not choose to consume the Rabbit.

Snake—Dragon

If the possessive Snake will allow the autonomous Dragon to leave the lair from time to time, this pairing can proceed smoothly. If the Snake constricts the Dragon's movement, there will be difficulties.

Snake—Snake

This is a lovely relationship steeped in beauty, elegance, and otherworldly knowledge. Nonetheless, a double dose of the passive, negative, feminine yin energy leaves these two always wanting the other to take the lead. Expect a long, contemplative courtship.

Snake—Horse

Mutual respect and intense physical attraction make this a workable union. However, the hurdles that the Horse must jump are external, in contrast to the Snake's mainly internal world. This can erect a fence between the two souls.

Snake—Goat

These two very yin souls need to attach themselves to a strong wagon that does much of the pulling for them. A chilly relationship with too much emotional distance and no one to take the lead.

Snake—Monkey

These unlikely soul mates have the potential to celebrate a golden wedding anniversary. Equally matched in both guile and allure, the Snake and the Monkey will seldom tire of their intense physical attraction to each other. However, beware of infidelities that can derail the union.

Snake—Rooster

This is a winning combination of wisdom and work. The philosophical Snake and the industrious Rooster speak a common language of conservatism, method, and physical appearance. Still, the Rooster is an early riser and the Snake prefers to languish until noon.

Snake—Dog

These two souls never run out of interesting topics to discuss and are first-rate friends. They both seek to understand the metaphysics of life and tend to be multi-sensorial. They will enjoy many hours together delving into otherworldly knowledge.

Snake—Pig

While both are decent and deeply feeling souls, the Snake and the Pig remain in polarized opposition. The Pig judges the Snake to be less scrupulous and inferior to him, while the Snake quickly tires of the Pig's Pollyannaish naiveté. This drives a wedge between the two.

CHAPTER 23

鼠牛虎兔龍蛇馬羊猴鷄犬猪

HORSE HOTTIE

Jan 25, 1906 to Feb 12, 1907: Fire Horse
Feb 11, 1918 to Jan 31, 1919: Earth Horse
Jan 30, 1930 to Feb 16, 1931: Metal Horse
Feb 15, 1942 to Feb 4, 1943: Water Horse
Feb 3, 1954 to Jan 23, 1955: Wood Horse
Jan 21, 1966 to Feb 8, 1967: Fire Horse
Feb 7, 1978 to Jan 27, 1979: Earth Horse
Jan 27, 1990 to Feb 14, 1991: Metal Horse
Feb 12, 2002 to Jan 31, 2003: Water Horse
Jan 31, 2014 to Feb 18, 2015: Wood Horse
Needs: communication
Hates: sulking, pouting
Turn-ons: gourmet food, fine wine, travel
Turnoffs: snobbery

The friendly Horse needs social relationships and absolute freedom to maneuver through love's pastures. This independent seventh sign of the Zodiac needs a lover who stimulates their mind and appreciates their wit. These physically active and quick-witted lovers are charming, independent, and decisive. Both male and female Horses prefer to be on the move, with places to go and people to see. Horses rule the life palace of sexuality and possess a potent libido. Elegant, witty, and lusty, those born into Horse years like sex and a lot of it.

Horse souls value their freedom absolutely. They are physically attractive, intense, and enchanting lovers who are difficult to tame. They are also natural leaders, and idealistic and humanitarian in character. Those who love a Horse must also be lovers of challenge and adventure. Sentimental, impatient, and ardent for love, Horses seek to overwhelm their partners—and be thunderstruck themselves in the process. These souls can be infatuate and fall prey to sudden attractions. Passionate, and vulnerable to just the right smile, the Horse lives according to the rhythms of their heart. They love with their entire being and are never short on conversation. Eager to hear and discuss their lover's opinions, active and energetic Horses are affectionate and entertaining companions.

It is difficult for Horses to maintain interest in a day-to-day, mundane existence. A Horse's dream honeymoon is akin to a week of episodes on the Travel Channel. Nothing could be more romantic for the Horse than expeditions, adventure, and the exotic. Their sensual proclivities come from afar as well, and draw them to distant times, foreign cultures, and other worlds. Whether a solo traveler, a philosopher, or a research scientist, the Horse crosses borders—literally and metaphorically. The concept of thinking "outside the box" is decisively Horse-like. In the spiritual, mental, and physical realms, Horse-year souls reject the commonplace.

The Chinese word for Horse—"wu"—also means high noon, and it is during the midday hours between 11 a.m. and 1 p.m. that love and sex rule for the Horse. The lunchtime quickie was tailor-made for the hot-blooded Horse!

If your man was born into a Horse year:

Whether he is a stallion in full gallop or a wobbly young colt, the Horse man has a "certain something" that entices females. Maybe it's the way he moves so gracefully, whether he's on a stage or in a martial arts competition. Whatever the specifics, this man is pure, unadulterated yang energy. Along with the Goat, he rules the heavenly palace of sexuality (the Horse is the representation of the masculine yang force and the Goat is the representation of the feminine yin force), and together they form the karmic palace of unions.

The hidden Elemental stem in the Horse-year branch is Fire, which creates an urge for rapid resolution in the male Horse's sexuality. He is susceptible to love at first sight and can be capricious in love. Impulsive, ardent, and frank, Horse men tend to be involved with many projects at the same time—and this can also include women! Powerful romantic emotions can temporarily outweigh logic and put blinders on the Horse. Although he is straightforward and open about his fickleness, he nevertheless seems to have more than his share of short-lived relationships.

Horse men abhor restrictions, and sexually speaking they march to the beat of their own drummer. Their formidable intelligence rejects outmoded beliefs, and they balk at convention. This makes for an adventuresome lover, impassioned and invested—body, mind, and soul—in his beloved. This is a man who knows how to treat a woman, and her subsequent relations with other men may seem dull. He's a hard act to follow. Similar to his Dog-year brothers, the Horse male seeks his soul mate in this life. He is sometimes accused of looking for love in all the wrong places, but at least he's looking. Communication and variety are the sexual spice of his life.

This is a man who looks for a high quality in his physical relations. His approach to sex is sensual and affectionate, and he is capable of tuning out the world and everything around him once he begins to make love. Similar to his Tiger brothers, he is attracted to glamorous, unavailable, and even slightly dangerous women. This man is a competitor at heart, so romantic conquest has a special appeal to him. Emotional stability in a lover turns him on, and an intelligent woman who also possesses physical beauty is a recipe for romantic nirvana. Mutual trust between him and his lover, combined with complete personal freedom, is the glue that will hold his love relationship strong.

Whether a renowned archaeologist on an excavation, a paranormal investigator substantiating a haunting, or a war correspondent reporting from the front lines, the Horse man craves exotic, unusual, and exciting professions—and women. He has a pronounced weakness for intelligent, beautiful, and aggressive partners. He also needs to feel admired by his lover, and will thrive with a partner who reinforces his self-confidence, who believes in his projects, and who takes responsibility for her own happiness.

The Horse man's honesty is forthright and occasionally shocking. He has no problem running down the complete list of his past relationships, replete with sexual tidbits that his current partner may or may not appreciate hearing. It's his way of "bonding" with his current love and saying that he considers their relationship potentially serious. In his mind, his candid confessions clear the romantic slate and enable him to start anew.

Even when he has found the woman of his dreams, the Horse man will need to retain the feeling of remaining free and unattached. Despite his sincere commitment to his lover and family, the truth is that he easily becomes bored and needs new experiences as much as he needs oxygen. In addition, he is always ready, willing, and able go on trips, cruises, expeditions, stake-outs, whatever—as long as he's in forward motion and there is something for his fertile mind to discover. Novelist Christopher Morely summed up the essence of the male Horse eloquently when he wrote, "There is only one success, to be able to spend your life in your own way."

If your woman was born into a Horse year:

Whether a majestic mare or a feisty filly, the female Horse tends to throw herself impetuously into tumultuous love affairs. These reckless choices can leave her love life strewn with broken affairs and less than fulfilling relationships. She is such a strong yang female that weaker men may be threatened by her uncompromising independence and dynamic personality. Akin to her equally strong Tiger sisters, the Horse woman must hold her lover in very high esteem; she can be caustically critical and sarcastic with a man who falls short of her expectations. Also, she is not a "touchy-feely" woman, and her lack of stereotypical feminine sympathies can make her a little insecure regarding her femininity at times.

Thus, the Horse woman's love life is rarely a smooth or easy one. In her dreams she secretly longs for a chivalrous, handsome prince to whisk her away on his steed; but alas, romantic love may continue to elude her. In addition, the idea of giving up her personal freedom for love seems ridiculous. A marriage license is seen as a necessary evil and even an obstacle to true love in the eyes of many female Horses. Even when she knuckles under to societal pressure and opts for the conventional couple's life, this is a lady who will insist that her partner give her a very long rope. Her lover should never forget how stubbornly she defends her personal freedom and know that she cannot sacrifice liberation for love. She needs a comunicative, energetic, and self-assured lover. The noble Tiger man (in trine with the Horse) is one of the few males virile and assertive enough to handle this thoroughbred. When she finally finds that strong man who can appreciate her finer qualities and not view her as a rival, she will kick up her heels and give him the ride of his life!

The North Pole position, sometimes called the "pair of flying ducks," suits her style nicely. She sits backwards and straddles her man's erect penis as she slowly lowers and allows it to penetrate her vagina. She is then in a position to direct the speed and depth of intercourse. She may also gently cup her lover's testicles, stimulate him anally, or massage the erogenous zone located between his anus and testicles. Her lover can relax and enjoy himself fully while she takes the lead and satisfies her assertive needs. As an extra bonus, her man has an incredibly erotic view of her beautiful back, buttocks, and waist curves—some of her best attributes.

Compatibilities

Romantically, the best match for the Horse is with those born during Tiger or Horse years; however, their soul mate is found with the artistic Goat. Be cautious in love relationships with the Rat and Ox.

Horse (+ yang):

Soul mate to—Goat

In trine with—Tiger, Dog

In opposition to—Rat

Combatant to—Ox

In kind with—Goat

Resolving karma with—Rooster

Steed—Monkey

Peach blossom—Rabbit

Horse—Rat

Interestingly, despite their direct opposition, these souls tend to attract one another frequently. However, Rats need an understanding ear to listen to their ideas while Horses are too preoccupied with their own dreams and ambitions. This relationship can end in bitterness.

Horse—Ox

The Horse would rather be anyplace except home. This is nothing less than treason to the Ox, who holds the family circle in such reverence. The Horse mistakenly interprets the Ox's stability as authoritarianism, and neither sign has the foggiest idea of how the other thinks and feels.

Horse—Tiger

These two are natural friends and lovers. Each supports the other in their mutual pursuit of making this world a better place. Both are physically active, athletic, and in forward "yang" motion.

Horse—Rabbit

The Rabbit doesn't mind staying home and enjoying his privacy while the Horse is out conquering new pastures. This pairing makes an enjoyable friendship and amiable union.

Horse—Dragon

This union could end in an ego clash of epic proportions, as both the Horse and the Dragon vie for attention and audience approval. These two will seldom acquiesce to share the limelight, and neither will compromise with the other. This is a difficult relationship.

Horse—Snake

Mutual respect and intense physical attraction make this a workable union. However, the hurdles that the Horse yearns to jump are external, while the Snake is mainly preoccupied with internal concerns. This difference in temperament can erect a fence between the two.

Horse—Horse

Similar to their Tiger brothers and sisters, two Horse souls are just too much of a good thing. The double yang and Fire Element can contribute to a virtual stampede through life. If these two independent souls team up, they will probably spend a lot of time apart.

Horse—Goat

These two soul mates compliment each other perfectly. The Horse is the very personification of the positive, yang day-force, and the Goat is the absolute essence of the negative, yin night-force. Together these two make up a perfect whole.

Horse—Monkey

This is a relationship that challenges every bit of the Monkey's ingenuity and artfulness. If the clever Monkey can convince the Horse that life with her will be unique, this can work quite nicely.

Horse—Rooster

This is a difficult pairing of energies in that neither feels a strong enough bond to make any sacrifices for the other. The Rooster's fussiness leaves the Horse feeling tense and nervous. This is an apathetic relationship in friendship and in love.

Horse—Dog

The Dog and the Horse comprise a remarkable couple. These two souls adore each other and speak the same language of feelings, family, and fairness. These exceptional humanitarians may very well find themselves in the limelight.

Horse—Pig

Surprisingly, the normally peace-loving Pig can become antagonistic and quarrelsome when paired with the Horse. The Pig feels compelled to correct the Horse and generally rains on the Horse's parade.

CHAPTER 24

鼠牛虎兔龍蛇馬羊猴鶏犬猪

GO-GO GOAT

Feb 13, 1907 to Feb 1, 1908: Fire Goat
Feb 1, 1919 to Feb 19, 1920: Earth Goat
Feb 17, 1931 to Feb 5, 1932: Metal Goat
Feb 5, 1943 to Jan 24, 1944: Water Goat
Jan 24, 1955 to Feb 11, 1956: Wood Goat
Feb 9, 1967 to Jan 29, 1968: Fire Goat
Jan 28, 1979 to Feb 15, 1980: Earth Goat
Feb 15, 1991 to Feb 3, 1992: Metal Goat
Feb 1, 2003 to Jan 21, 2004: Water Goat
Feb 19, 2015 to Feb 7, 2016: Wood Goat
Needs: flexibility
Hates: responsibility, cruelty
Turn-ons: the oceanfront, secluded beaches
Turnoffs: physical labor

Skipping from one romantic cloud to the next, the intelligent, creative, and insecure Goat is the artistic lover of the Zodiac. Sensitive, kind, and generous (sometimes to a fault), those souls born into Goat years are warmhearted, disorganized, and extremely vulnerable emotionally. They are also changeable free spirits who love social gatherings, stimulating conversation, and interesting people. From the Goat point of view, the ideal relationship entails being able to be creative and enjoy the beautiful and aesthetic sides of life while their partner manages the mundane, day-to-day aspects of life. Beautiful surroundings, fine dining, the ballet, art, music, and poetry are what romance is made of for Goats. On the other hand, hours spent filling out income tax forms is sure to kill any romantic notions.

Goats are creative and complex, and this applies to their sexual psychology as well. Being essentially yin, whether male or female, Goats are romantically fickle: they are prone to infatuations and obsessions, but they also tend to be rather dependent and like the feeling of being cared for. Additionally, they prefer to be sure of their lover's affection before approaching physical pleasures. Gentle in spirit, the Goat desires a peaceful spot to love undisturbed and unhurried. A beautiful environment is especially important to their sexual relations. This sensitive and unobtrusive soul has impeccable taste and uses this ability to create the comfortable and inviting love nest they so crave. Goats wrote the book on creating romantic ambiance. From Lava lamps to candles, bubble baths to sensual massage, Goats rule the boudoir!

In love and in sex, the easy-going Goat can give a great deal, but will expect much in return. In sexual relations with these hypersensitive souls, the key words are appropriateness and delicacy. This soft heart needs a stable partner able to take the reins. Goats are at their sexual peak during the early afternoon hours between 1 p.m. and 3 p.m.

If your man was born into a Goat year:

Similar to his Goat sisters, the Goat man lives in an inner world rich with imagination. Love and emotional attachment are the lifeblood to him, and he looks at all of life through the filter of his heart. Capricious and changeable in love, he tries to be sexually faithful, but it doesn't seem reasonable to him that he should go the rest of his life denying himself the pleasures of so many beautiful women. This rascal can and will juggle multiple relationships, as women are drawn to his boyish good looks and feminine yin side. His "fatal attraction" for women means that his partner will have to stay on her toes to keep him on her porch. However, his partner will never be entirely sure of what is going on inside his head, relationship-wise. She may be the last to know of his dissatisfaction, and once he has made the decision to move on he will do so with a rapidity that can leave his partner shocked and dismayed. She will seldom be able to convince him to linger or reconsider.

As a lover, the Goat man is sensitive, charming, and capable of uncommon tenderness and good manners. The early stages of romantic love make him feel vibrantly alive like nothing else. Anxious for ecstasy and an expert in the art of lovemaking, he knows how to keep his lover's interest. In the bedroom he is a giver rather than a taker, and nothing turns him on more than the sound of his lover moaning with pleasure. Spontaneity and fantasy are the most apparent aspects of his sexual appetite, and he is free from sexual hang-ups or inhibitions of any kind. His sexual intuition borders on the psychic. Indeed, he seems to know most women better than they know themselves. In addition, he is a master in the sensual arts as well as in the esoteric aspects of sex; Eastern spiritual cultivation through sexual practices interests him greatly. Refusing to accept outdated sexual dogma, he likes to experiment. Put bluntly, his sexual maxim is, "It's all good." Bedtime is rarely for sleeping with this penetrating, poetic, and perceptive lover.

If your woman was born into a Goat year:

The female Goat is an absolute romantic. In concert with the rest of her life, love and sex for the Goat woman begin with a slow dance. The Goat woman is emotionally wired for love and can only do without male company for so long. Emotional, vulnerable, and fantasy-prone, the Goat woman is all about the preliminaries. She is a true sensual "empath," and her sexuality is more mystical than primal. This is a woman who doesn't engage in sex merely for carnal knowledge, but also as a means to express her spiritual side and artistic spirit. She is an artistic and poetic lover who intuitively senses what her partner wants and needs. Along with the Horse, this 100 percent yin female rules the life palace of sexuality and can unleash a waterfall of sensual treats. The Goat woman personifies the sex kitten of days gone by, the woman for whom men have been known to swim oceans and go bankrupt. Men in general tend to find her utterly female.

In love, but especially in sex, she exhibits a strong dichotomy. On the one hand, she firmly believes in the concept of soul mates and true love, and her temperament craves the perfect relationship in which she is unconditionally loved and so loves in return. This is the idealistic, sentimental, and empathetic side of her heart, the side that enables her to devote herself to a man completely. (Less committed partners may feel overwhelmed by this total dedication and undivided interest.) On the other hand, while her inner temperament seeks harmony, love, and bonding, her character sometimes speaks quite differently: The Goat female requires financial ease and material comforts, and her warm feelings will quickly turn to stone with a cheap or penny-pinching partner. She can generally tolerate just about anything except financial distress.

Her romantic heart needs to be handled like fragile rice paper. A careless comment, an apathetic look, or a brusque gesture can be enough to send her on a perma-pout. This is a woman who has the ability to take the art of sulking to new heights. Additionally, she needs overt and concrete demonstrations of her man's love. Romantic trappings are the first phase of her sexual psychology—flowers, elegant dinners, and jewelry are at the top of her wish list.

While earnestly fickle, she is all woman. A surefire way to give your Goat lady a taste of heaven is by using the favorite "peach blossom" position. In this, she lies on her back and raises her legs up toward her head. Her man penetrates her as she brings her legs to rest on his shoulders, which frees him to hold onto either one or both of her legs as they move together with his thrusts. In this position she can stimulate her own clitoris using her favorite touch and bring herself to orgasm. This is also a huge turn-on for her lover who can watch her from above. With a quick change of her leg position, she may bend her knees and bring them close to her breasts. With both hands gently holding her legs back, her lover can use his penis first to thrust into her vagina, then externally along her clitoris, and then vaginally once more. He continues this until she reaches orgasm.

Compatibilities

Romantically, the best match for the Goat is with those born during Rabbit or Pig years; however their true soul mate is found with the enthusiastic Horse. Be cautious in love relationships with the Ox and Rat.

Goat (- Yin):

Soul mate to—Horse

In trine with—Rabbit, Pig

In opposition to—Ox

Combatant to—Rat

In kind with—Horse

Resolving karma with—Dog

Steed—Snake

Peach blossom—Rat

Goat—Rat

This relationship is a difficult one. The Rat is an early riser and the Goat is not. These two seem to have many interests in common, but the way in which each views the world is radically different. This pairing makes better friends than lovers.

Goat—Ox

If one says black, the other says white. These two polarized opposites can make sparks fly with their radically different temperaments and opinions. Oxen are predictable and responsible, but Goats experience this behavior as confining and even tyrannical.

Goat—Tiger

This combination of souls can have its pleasant moments, but more often than not, friction is the usual result. The fearless Tiger will bulldoze right over the sensitive Goat. These two have fun as social acquaintances, but marriage may prove to be too difficult for them.

Goat—Rabbit

In their quest to find and create beauty in this life, the Rabbit and the Goat form a melodious union. These two best friends walk hand-in-hand through a world of aesthetics, culture, and refinement.

Goat—Dragon

This unusual pairing can work nicely if the Dragon doesn't overwhelm the Goat. Although they can enjoy a strong and lasting attraction, the Goat will have trouble keeping her balance through the Dragon's changeable moods.

Goat—Snake

These two very "yin" souls need to attach themselves to a strong wagon that does much of the pulling for them. This is a chilly relationship with too much emotional distance and no one to take the lead.

Goat—Horse

These two soul mates compliment each other perfectly. The Horse is the very personification of the positive, yang day-force, and the Goat is the absolute essence of the negative, yin night-force. Together these two make up one perfect whole.

Goat—Goat

This pair is a picnic amongst the clouds. These two good Samaritans enjoy each other's company and share a sensitivity to beauty and balance. No competition exists between these fortunate and romantic souls. Two Goats should be very cautious in handling their own finances, though.

Goat—Monkey

The Goat and the Monkey are immediately attracted to one another and get along famously—for a while. The Monkey enjoys the Goat's fortunate financial position until the price becomes too high to pay. While a rare occurrence, the Monkey has the ability to con or swindle the Goat.

Goat—Rooster

This is a challenging relationship of leisure clashing with hard work. The fact that the Rooster prods and pushes the Goat to be more productive is not conducive to harmony between these two.

Goat—Dog

Both souls tend to be pessimistic and prone to melancholy, and this double dose of cynicism does neither the anxious Dog nor the depressive Goat any good. The Dog herds the Goat into places he has no desire to go, which can out the billy goat's horns.

Goat—Pig

A loving and symbiotic relationship of courtesy and respect exists between these two gentle souls. The Goat teaches the Pig about romance, and in turn learns temperance from the Pig.

CHAPTER 25

鼠牛虎兔龍蛇馬羊猴鷄犬猪

MARATHON MONKEY

Feb 2, 1908 to Jan 21, 1909: Earth Monkey
Feb 20, 1920 to Feb 7, 1921: Metal Monkey
Feb 6, 1932 to Jan 25, 1933: Water Monkey
Jan 25, 1944 to Feb 12, 1945: Wood Monkey
Feb 12, 1956 to Jan 30, 1957: Fire Monkey
Jan 30, 1968 to Feb 16, 1969: Earth Monkey
Feb 16, 1980 to Feb 4, 1981: Metal Monkey
Feb 4, 1992 to Jan 22, 1993: Water Monkey
Jan 22, 2004 to Feb 8, 2005: Wood Monkey
Feb 8, 2016 to Jan 27, 2017: Fire Monkey

Needs: versatility

Hates: control

Turn-ons: Las Vegas, Atlantic City, casinos

Turnoffs: humorless people

The youthful and clever Monkey is the "eternal child" of the Eastern Zodiac, and brings a sense of fun and innocence into the bedroom. Smart, multifaceted, and blessed with a delicious sense of humor, Monkeys are sexually complicated and wear a romantic veil of many colors. These irrepressible souls are restless, enterprising, and very sexual. Mischievous and high-spirited, the Monkey's love liaisons are characterized by imagination, ingenuity, and resourcefulness. Monkeys are versatile and amusing lovers, but can have difficulties in relationships due to a secret underlying mistrust of others. For this reason, communication is important for a Monkey, both in and out of the bedroom. Both males and females thrive with a calm, stable, and intuitive lover.

Restless and sexually curious, Monkeys possess an effervescent character that infatuates easily, but quickly becomes bored. Their unequivocal need for sexual variety means that many Monkeys chose to remain unmarried on principal, even if they are involved in a long-term relationship. To a Monkey, a ring around the finger can feel like a rope around the neck. Versatile, curious, and easily bored, these performance-oriented "yang" lovers need mentally sharp partners who stimulate their minds and therefore their bodies. Their sexual qi peaks during the late afternoon hours between 3 p.m. and 5 p.m.

If your man was born into a year of the Monkey:

The creative and paradoxical Monkey male lives in a fantasy world of sensory and fleshly delights. This playful and amusing lover is a fun and supremely social animal. His love life resembles the ebb and flow of the tides, as it is constantly wavering back and forth. "He loves me, he loves me not"—these are the mixed signals pondered by most of his lovers. On the more positive side, he looks for a strong friendship component in whatever relationship he's in.

The core of his relationship problems lies in his absolute refusal to surrender his freedom. But he's torn: He needs companionship and doesn't enjoy being alone; however, similar to his Horse brothers, he is prone to infatuations, and can fall in (and out) of love effortlessly. Stability and monogamy can be very challenging for him. This is a soul who will always prefer a casual union over a traditional marriage. However, regardless of whether he chooses to content himself with one-night stands or takes the plunge into marriage, his love remains an innocent and youthful one.

His sexual appetite is more than adequate, but it is only one small part of his kaleidoscopic psycho-social make up. He enjoys both the thrill of the chase and the courtship phase in his poker game of sex. "Sometimes you get lucky, sometimes you don't," is his motto. Love and romance are a numbers game to this mercurial man, and he believes that he must meet a certain number of females for his winning percentage of compatibility to come up. Thus is the Monkey male's casino of love.

Monkey men can be particularly attracted to inaccessible women (married, older, younger). Often, this is subconscious behavior that helps him guard against the possibility that someone might ask him to surrender his freedom. However, it *is* possible for an extraordinary woman to bring his love hunt to a halt. The woman who captures his heart will be mysterious, non possessive, and will always keep him guessing. If he can find a partner who will allow him to act out his fantasies on their private stage, he just might get hooked. The temptress who ensnares this versatile animal will be well-rewarded with an enthusiastic and prolific lover.

Sexual acrobatics are a Monkey male specialty, so the "inner door" position is likely to be a favorite. In this, his woman lies face down on the bed with just the top half of her upper body touching. While he holds her legs he penetrates her from behind, and she raises her buttocks to enjoy the sensations on her labia. For more sensation, she can tighten her vaginal muscles as he penetrates, and relax as he withdraws.

If your woman was born into a year of the Monkey:

The Monkey female's love life resembles the complex maze of an English garden. With each twist and turn through the hedges, the lost lover becomes less and less able to find the exit. Quandary and contradiction are the cornerstones of her love life. The clever and optimistic Monkey woman is eternally on the lookout for romantic opportunities and forever actively searching for her prince charming. However, once she finds him, she realizes that *wanting* was better than *having*. The jungle of romantic fantasy always looks greener on the other side. When disappointment sets in she becomes a very different creature from her normally jocular self, and disenchantment regarding her partner can quickly turn into contempt. However, she hates this negative and critical side of her personality: it drains her energy and makes for one very miserable Monkey maiden. It is yet another reason why she wishes to keep her freedom to end an affair if necessary. Unpredictability and inconsistency are her greatest obstacles in love, and she has no problem professing one thing and doing another.

During the courtship stage, romance is a necessity for her, but she is never in a hurry to marry or commit. She enjoys long engagements as they insure both intellectual compatibility and friendship.

Actually, this is not a woman who is easily overtaken by passion—she likes to keep things "light." She will insist on sharing her bed with a "friend," and places more importance on the friendship than on romantic frills. She is slow to warm up sexually, and while she doesn't particularly care for romantic props (and even finds them silly), to a certain extent she needs them to help her transition from stark reality to a state of relaxation. So choose your candles, music, and pillows—your Monkey lady awaits! However, you should be warned that if she hasn't made a mental connection with you, there is no ambiance on earth that will put her in the mood.

The "yin/yang communion" position is a great one for the Monkey woman because it will satisfy her casual sexual style and her need to merge sex with friendship. In this position, the woman sits facing her lover on his lap, straddles his erect penis, and allows it to penetrate her deeply. This position is ideal for passionate kissing as well as a feeling of friendship and playfulness.

Compatibilities

Romantically, the best match for the Monkey is with those born during Rat or Dragon years; however, their true soul mate is found with the sage Snake. Be cautious in love relationships with the Tiger and Pig.

Monkey (+ yang):

Soul mate to—Snake

In trine with—Rat, Dragon

In Opposition to—Tiger

Combatant to—Pig

In kind with—Rooster

Resolving karma with—Pig

Steed—Tiger

Peach blossom—Rooster

Monkey—Rat

Sexuality is a pleasure and a gift between Rats and Monkeys. These two love each other and are not bashful about it. Nights of love intertwined with intellectual stimulation await this pair.

Monkey—Ox

Because of their self-sufficient and practical nature, love and sex are important, but not absolutely essential to Oxen. This dampens the Monkey's enthusiasm and often results in resentment.

Monkey—Tiger

These two opposite souls distrust each other. The fact that the Monkey is capable of playing tricks and gaining confidences sets the Tiger's nerves on edge.

Monkey—Rabbit

The Rabbit doesn't like to assume responsibility for the outcome of any situation, and hence usually passes the buck to the capable Monkey. The Monkey can't resist tricking the Rabbit, but the Rabbit is prepared to make a quick getaway.

Monkey—Dragon

These two compatible souls flow together naturally and are kindred spirits. Both bring to this union new and unanticipated methods of looking at and dealing with life. The Dragon and Monkey have an excellent chance for an enduring relationship.

Monkey—Snake

These unlikely soul mates will seldom tire of their intense physical attraction to each other. If the Snake becomes too stingy, however, this can make the Monkey depressed.

Monkey—Horse

This is a relationship that challenges every bit of the Monkey's ingenuity and artfulness. If the clever Monkey can convince the Horse that life with them will be unique and exciting, this pairing can work quite nicely.

Monkey—Goat

The Goat and the Monkey are immediately attracted to one another and get along famously—for a while. The Monkey enjoys the Goat's fortunate financial position, until having to follow the Goat's rules becomes too high a price to pay.

Monkey—Monkey

This is another harmonious same-sign match. These two souls are a handful together and a carnival of ideas and fun. There should be caution regarding third parties entering the union.

Monkey—Rooster

This is a pairing that can bring rewards to both sides. The lively debates between these two cause others to label it a love/hate relationship, but the relationship actually works admirably for both.

Monkey—Dog

The Monkey is one of the few signs who can lift the Dog out of his frequent bouts with doom and gloom. The Monkey offers the Dog friendship and love, as well as the much-needed ability to see life as a comedy.

Monkey—Pig

Considering the surprising regularity with which these two souls come together, the natural assumption would be that they are compatible. This is rarely the case, as the tricky Monkey can't resist misleading the naive Pig.

CHAPTER 26

鼠牛虎兔龍蛇馬羊猴鷄犬猪

ROUGH-AND-READY ROOSTER

Jan 22, 1909 to Feb 9, 1910: Earth Rooster
Feb 8, 1921 to Jan 27, 1922: Metal Rooster
Jan 26, 1933 to Feb 13, 1934: Water Rooster
Feb 13, 1945 to Feb 1, 1946: Wood Rooster
Jan 31, 1957 to Feb 17, 1958: Fire Rooster
Feb 17, 1969 to Feb 5, 1970: Earth Rooster
Feb 5, 1981 to Jan 24, 1982: Metal Rooster
Jan 23, 1993 to Feb 9, 1994: Water Rooster
Feb 9, 2005 to Jan 28, 2006: Wood Rooster
Jan 28, 2017 to Feb 15, 2018: Fire Rooster
Needs: respect
Hates: weakness
Turn-ons: control
Turnoffs: hypersensitivity

The appearance-conscious Rooster has an appetite for pageantry, especially in the bedroom. Both male and female Roosters love to socialize and adore adornment and finery. Their lively and outgoing sexual manner is as candid as their speech. Confident, industrious, and slightly sadistic, Roosters are best suited to relationships over which they have complete control.

The assertive Rooster needs a strong and self-assured partner whom they can both respect and dominate.

The Rooster's core traits of attention, observance, and scrutiny translate sexually into forbidden worlds, always potentially perverse and sometimes bordering on the sordid. The Rooster's sexual tastes, preferences, and imaginative scenarios can be shocking to some partners, yet relished by others. A good "fit" in a partner is important to Roosters, as they tend to push the limits of their sexuality and will always refuse to be confined to the mores of society.

If your man was born into a Rooster year:

Whether a cocky military man, a CEO, or a mechanical engineer, the Rooster male makes love with great determination, keeping his eyes fixed ever forward on the goal of ultimate pleasure. This is a conservative yet flirtatious man who presents an open and confident disposition. The Rooster man's love partner will need some proficiency and sexual credentials to capture his heart. These are men who thrive on compliments and have an emotional and possessive nature in matters of the heart. Because of their restless anxiety and impatience, Rooster men tend to be attracted to powerful and slightly dangerous women. Passion, perversion, and excess are what this rough-and-ready lover secretly craves.

According to Chinese legend, the Rooster male is extremely sexual, very fertile, and may have an above average number of children. He is essentially a conservative soul with a "yin" nature, so public displays of affection are generally not his cup of tea. Despite his reserved tendencies, however, this is one powder keg of a passionate lover! Any females who plan to hook up with this laser beam of a personality should know what they're getting themselves into.

Sexually, the Rooster man has a taste for sado-masochistic sex and role play. Master and slave is his game: taking his woman to the brink of orgasm, and then withholding her pleasure—only to bring her back to the edge to beg for more. This man likes drama in the bedroom, so a prudish or hung-up partner will surely send him packing. He prefers his sex powerful and forceful, and his woman submissive and sick with love for him. This is a man whose ideal lover is a myriad of different women—an independent businesswoman, angelic mother, and a supremely naughty lover all rolled into one.

The "butterfly clings to branch" position is a favorite for the Rooster male. In this, the woman lies face down on the bed with her arms outstretched in front of her, her buttocks raised, and her legs tucked beneath. She inhales and constricts her vaginal muscles tightly as he enters, then relaxes her muscles and exhales as he withdraws. If the woman's hair is long, her Rooster lover may gently bundle it in his hand, grasping it firmly yet delicately as he would fine silk. This feeling of being in control sexually will arouse him greatly. Once the Rooster's lover agrees to play the sexual games he proposes, she will find him a loyal, steadfast, and attentive lover.

On the more sordid side, tenderness isn't the Rooster man's strong point, and secretly he can enjoy being a little punishing with his woman. Playful spanking is a huge turn-on for the Rooster male, as is any form of control or domination. If his partner is amenable, he may take her over his lap and spank her buttocks just hard enough for them to turn slightly red, awakening and reviving her nerve endings. This "dry bath," or "patting," as the Taoists call it, is used in qi gong exercises to bring blood flow into various body parts. This high form of submissiveness can result in an explosive orgasm for the male Rooster. The rule is that he may never spank his lover unless she requests it. The goal for the Rooster man should be to cut down on the marathon foreplay, allow his woman to climax initially, and then bring her back to experience multiple orgasms over and over again.

All in all, the Rooster man is not an easy lover to live with. He needs a woman who is resilient enough and has a healthy enough ego to accept his intensity and emotional drama. Love him or hate him, but please do not ignore him.

If your woman was born into a Rooster year:

It is during the early evening cocktail hours of seduction between 5 p.m. and 7 p.m. that the Rooster woman struts her stuff. Endowed with a mysterious side, the Rooster woman is the original femme fatal. "Come into my parlor, said the spider to the fly" could be her sexual mantra. Secrecy, seduction, and even sadism are the weapons in her fascinating sexual arsenal. The balance of power is an important aspect in the Rooster female's sexual psyche—she likes her men to be at her mercy. Outside of the bedroom, this lady is conservative and family-oriented, and runs her home and business with the efficiency of a military general. But make no mistake about it: When you enter her boudoir, *she* is the one who is in control. The main Elements of her sexuality are dominance, control, and possessiveness. Behind closed doors, she relishes the role of a sexual dominatrix. She has a sexual will of iron and needs a strong lover to harness her intense passion and energy. She must have complete respect for her partner, as a weak lover or "yes-man" will bring out her most unbecoming characteristics.

Similar to her Rabbit sisters, she does not give her heart away easily. She is a perfectionist at heart, and unfortunately this carries over to her love life. She maintains some very high standards, and it is only to a partner who has won her respect that she will show her sentimental and more vulnerable side. On a darker note, her lover would be well-advised to know that jealousy and possessiveness constitute a significant part of her personality. The Rooster female has a suspicious nature is not above hiring a private detective to uncover any misrepresentations or undisclosed history. If betrayed, her vengeance will be quick and severe.

A satisfying position for both the Rooster female and her partner is the "North Pole" position, sometimes also called the "pair of flying ducks." In this, the woman sits backwards straddling her lover's erect penis. She then is in a position to gently cup the man's testicles, stimulate him anally, and generally be in complete control of the penile depth and pace of intercourse. She decides the next move, while her lover can relax and enjoy the erotic view of her beautiful back, buttocks, and waist curves.

The hidden Elemental stem in the Rooster-year branch is Metal, and this rigidity shows up in the Rooster woman's lovemaking style. The more sordid side of the female Rooster's sexual repertoire may contain such sadomasochistic props as whips, leather bondage accoutrements, and erotic costumes of various descriptions. The Rooster woman likes to probe and discover her lover's most intimate secrets. Pillow talk is a candid affair of confessions prompted by her own type of erotic "truth serum." If you desire a strong and direct partner, or enjoy power-exchanging, role-playing sex, the Rooster woman is for you!

Compatibilities

Romantically, the best match for the Rooster is with those born during Ox and Snake years; however, their true soul mate is found with the self-confident Dragon. Be cautious in love relationships with the Dog and Rabbit.

Rooster (- yang):

Soul mate to—Dragon

In trine with—Ox, Snake

In opposition to—Rabbit

Combatant to—Dog

In kind with—Monkey

Resolving karma with—Rat

Steed—Pig

Peach blossom—Horse

Rooster—Rat

Both Rats and Roosters like to talk, and this includes the bedroom where there will be lively discussions. The serious obstacle facing this couple is that both signs tend to be critical and outspoken when pointing out the other's shortcomings. The result can be a combative blood-fest of dissertation and argument, usually resulting in the Rat having hurt feelings. To make matters worse, these two are drawn together by a "resolving karma" relationship vibration. Good short-term sex, but a long-term relationship is not likely.

Rooster—Ox

These two signs are "in trine" and one of the best relationship matches. The conservative Ox delights in the company of the efficient Rooster, who brings passion and pepper to their sexual union. Whether it's a female Ox keeping the home fires burning for her scrappy Rooster husband, or a male Ox enjoying his "little firecracker" of a Rooster wife efficiently running their home, this is a match destined to last.

Rooster—Tiger

These two souls have problems communicating. The Tiger and the Rooster are both "skyrocket" personalities, and the union of these two can spark some memorable clashes. They are both domineering personalities, and the Rooster's sarcasm and know-it-all attitude quickly causes the Tiger to mutiny before jumping ship for new waters. More than likely this is an infatuate affair rather than a long-term relationship.

Rooster—Rabbit

These two souls are in direct opposition to each other. Despite any well-meaning efforts either of them may expend, this is not an auspicious relationship. If these two do get together the Rabbit is usually only along for the sexual ride. This is especially true if the Rabbit thinks the industrious Rooster can benefit them outside of the bedroom. The Rooster considers the Rabbit a weak partner and too easily hurt. This brings out the sadist in the Rooster, who will almost always play the "top" dominant sexual partner of the two.

Rooster—Dragon

Most Rooster/Dragon pairings have ties from other times and places, and thus form a true soul mate connection. The Dragon is yang to the Rooster's yin, and together they make a handsome and lively couple. The Rooster has the backbone and bravado to hold the interest of the unpredictable Dragon, while the Dragon is one of the few signs who can dominate and command the Rooster's respect. Together, these two rock each other's world!

Rooster—Snake

Similar to the Rooster and the Ox, the Rooster and Snake are "in trine" with each other and share a deep connection. The philosophical Snake and the industrious Rooster speak a common language of gradual accumulation, calculation, and attractive appearance. Both share a love of the arts and finer things in life. The Rooster is busier, more efficient, and more aggressive than the pensive, deep-thinking Snake, who remains the real power behind the throne.

Rooster—Horse

The Rooster and Horse are in a "peach blossom" relationship with each other, the kind responsible for torrid love affairs and emotional roller coaster rides. This is a love/hate relationship, so if love drama is what you seek, look no further! This intense romance connection can be the source of celebration or self-destruction. Despite the friction in the relationship, these two may have trouble disconnecting from each other.

Rooster—Goat

This is a challenging relationship of industry clashing with sloth. When the Rooster prods and pushes the Goat to be more productive, the Goat feels tyrannized and is likely to rebel.

Rooster—Monkey

This is an auspicious coupling that brings rewards to both sides. The lively debates between these two sometimes resemble a love/hate relationship, but it works well in the long run.

Rooster—Rooster

Whether showy Peacocks or gentle hens, these two souls will rarely cohabitate peacefully. The cliché of the cock fight is used to describe the interaction between two plucky Roosters.

Rooster—Dog

This is a difficult combination of energies. Should a verbal brawl break out between these two, take cover! Each sign antagonizes the other, and a relationship is likely to bring out the worst in both personalities.

Rooster—Pig

This is a blissful relationship with sincere admiration between the two. The Rooster benefits from the Pig's wisdom and presence of mind, while the Pig offers the Rooster respect and admiration.

鼠牛虎兔龍蛇馬羊猴鶏犬猪

DOG-GIE STYLE

Feb 10, 1910 to Jan 29, 1911: Metal Dog
Jan 28, 1922 to Feb 15, 1923: Water Dog
Feb 14, 1934 to Feb 3, 1935: Wood Dog
Feb 2, 1946 to Jan 21, 1947: Fire Dog
Feb 18, 1958 to Feb 7, 1959: Earth Dog
Feb 6, 1970 to Jan 26, 1971: Metal Dog
Jan 25, 1982 to Feb 12, 1983: Water Dog
Feb 10, 1994 to Jan 30, 1995: Wood Dog
Jan 29, 2006 to Feb 3, 2007: Fire Dog
Feb 16, 2018 to Feb 4, 2019: Earth Dog
Needs: reassurance
Hates: unfairness, abandonment
Turn-ons: firesides, fur rugs, log cabins
Turnoffs: one-night stands

Anxiety, loyalty, and protectiveness characterize these watchful worriers of the Chinese Zodiac, and they need much more reassurance than they would ever admit from their love partners. Trust and emotional attachment is always serious business to the Dog, and they are rarely "off-duty," even in the bedroom. A fast-starter the Dog is not, as they are hesitant to throw caution to the wind and abandon themselves to ecstasy.

Being under the influence of overpowering emotions is a scary place for most Dogs to be, and their ingrained suspicions are a huge obstacle for them to overcome. Cautious and serious regarding love, the Dog needs a trustworthy lover who is capable of strong attachments and commitment. A soul mate will understand the necessity of handling the pup's tender heart with kid gloves.

Known for complete loyalty toward their friends and loved ones (and vengefulness toward the enemies of their loved ones), in the realm of love and sex it's all or nothing, black or white. In the Dog's heart, you're either *in* or you're *out*. The Dog is a sincere, giving, and faithful lover, but their ever-present wariness means that they can have a sharp tongue and a tendency to jump to conclusions. They are experts in putting two and two together to come up with five. Hell hath no fury like a jealous Dog. The heart-wrenching howl of a betrayed or rejected Dog can make the bite from anyone else seem innocuous. Both male and female Dogs have difficulty letting go of relationships, and they lead the love parade when it comes to romantic obsessions and compulsions.

The most auspicious time for Dogs to make love is during the early evening hours of 7 p.m. to 9 p.m.

If your man was born into a Dog year:

Whether a servant or the president, Dog men are rescuers. They specialize in searching for the princess who can wear the glass slipper. Sometimes to the Dog man's downfall, the woman of his dreams is either a princess or a pauper, dignified or dejected. She will generally come from a high place in society—an achiever, powerful and brilliant—or she will be a downtrodden victim of fate relegated to the lowest ranks of society. Inaccessible women fascinate him, so the key to fanning his love fire is to return his love somewhat—but not entirely. If he feels that his woman's love is still to be won, he'll stand on his head and stack BB's for her. Masochism has a distinct fascination for Dog males. They will often attempt to champion and rescue troubled partners, but some of their queens can be very cruel taskmasters. Taken for granted and many times made a certified whipping boy, the Dog male may decide to stick with a relationship until his mental health is at stake. This is a man who is in the game of love for keeps.

His deeply ingrained sense of fairness produces a "tit for tat" sexuality and a desire for equality on a sexual level. This is a lover who can easily forget his own sexual needs and focus exclusively on those of his partner. He enjoys the courting period when making initial connections with lovers, and he is a generous and lavishly seductive lover. However, Dog men are some of the most suspicious creatures on the planet. You name it and he mistrusts it. Terrified of abandonment, the Dog man treads cautiously and covers himself with an emotional suit of armor.

In love, the Dog man likes stability and the familiar. He tends to cling to habits that reassure him, and this includes his choice in women. This is a soul who needs to be friends with his lover first. And not just friends with her, but also with her brother, mother, father—the whole clan. It is within this circle of familiarity, approval, and safety that the Dog man can emerge and declare his love. Love relationships later in life will be more fulfilling for both partners, as his emotional maturity develops later than his spiritual and intellectual facilities.

Sexually speaking, Dog men are highly aroused by the shape of a woman's buttocks, and will enjoy the rear entry positions. A Dog man will enjoy playfully surprising his lover from behind when she is on her hands and knees or lying face down with arms extended and small pillow elevating her buttocks. This is one of the best positions to hit her "G-spot," which is only a few finger widths deep inside the vagina (anterior wall). This position also allows either partner to reach around and have easy access to her clitoris. Not only is it extremely erotic for him to watch his woman stimulate herself while he is thrusting, but the contractions of her vagina as she orgasms will surely push him over the edge into ecstasy. The deliciously earthy Dog man can then begin the 9 x 10 thrust sequence (explained in further detail in Chapter 29).

His lover thinks she'll keep him!

If your woman was born in a Dog year:

Because the Dog woman has difficulty showing her feelings, it is up to her partner to coax her to open up and to relax. There are two faces to the Dog woman's sexual appetite: a cool, rather detached yang side that seeks to satisfy her physical and carnal lusts, and a more feminine yin side that gives and demands tenderness once her defenses have been lowered. The truth be told, she likes partners who are a little offbeat or odd.

A Dog woman remembers everything, and her memories of less-than-pleasant events can come back to haunt her at inopportune times. Looking beyond herself and putting past injuries to rest before approaching romance will put her on the road to sensual serenity. Faithful and reliable, the Dog woman has very rigid moral principles and a subconscious need to justify sex with love. This is why Dog women get very attached to partners once they have consummated the physical relationship. Serious and invested, a Dog woman needs a loyal partner by her side and in her bed. Remember that, despite her gender, she is essentially "yang," and needs a strong man resilient enough to face life's crises with her. For sizzling sex to happen, a Dog woman needs to trust her lover and believe that he will still be there in the morning. She knows how to keep a secret and will expect her partner to use the same discretion, keeping private what goes on between them in the bedroom.

In her search for her soul mate, the Dog woman seems to kiss a lot of frogs before her handsome prince arrives. She needs a partner who understands the deep anxiety and feeling of responsibility that fills her soul. This is a lady who will wither and shrivel up emotionally without tenderness; ironically, however, she herself can have trouble expressing affections. Similar to her Dog-year brothers, her emotional maturity develops later than her intellectual and spiritual abilities. This makes her a perfect candidate for later unions.

Similar to her Dog brothers, many Dog women express an attraction to experienced or older partners. Streetwise or powerful men who display some sort of authority or know-how turn her on.

The hidden Elemental stem in the Dog-year branch is Earth, and this earthiness shows up in the Dog woman's lovemaking style. She has a "take it or leave it" approach that can be either arousing or irritating, depending on her lover. Despite her protests that she is sexually open-minded, she doesn't have a reputation for variety and imagination in the bedroom. She generally prefers sex that is straightforward and simple; no-frills lovemaking is just fine with her and she will be quite happy with consistency. Basically, variety is less important to her than sexual security. However, this lusty lady is far from a cold fish, and her sexuality is deep and powerful. She has an air of artistry in bed, and once she begins practicing this her lover is rarely disappointed. She is hypersensitive to sounds of all kinds, however, so it is critical that she remove external noise and distractions from her bedroom. Trying to make love while the news blares in the background is a recipe for disaster. The only auditory stimulus a Dog lady wants is the sound of her partner moaning and begging for more.

In addition to her sense of hearing, the Dog woman's senses of smell and taste are also quite keen. She is one oral puppy! As a small child this may have lead to frequent flyer miles to the E.R. for ingesting medicines or non food items. But when she is a grown woman, this same proclivity can lead to fellatio nirvana for her man. Dog women are the queens of oral sex and have a natural flair for it. She can give her partner the most explosive orgasm of his life using the "lute string" position. Placing a pillow under her man's buttocks, she elevates his pelvis to a comfortable height, thus making him ready for his woman to go to work. Kneeling between his legs, she begins fellatio while reaching up to make small, stimulating circles on his nipples. The nipple play is very gentle at first, but increases in speed and intensity as the man approaches orgasm. Guaranteed to blow his mind!

Compatibilities

Both the Horse and the Tiger are excellent choices for enduring relationships, but the Dog's true soul mate is the Rabbit. Partnerships with the Dragon or the Rooster may be challenging.

Dog (+ yang):

Soul mate to—Rabbit

In trine with—Tiger, Horse

In opposition to—Dragon

Combatant to—Rooster

In kind with—Pig

Resolving karma with—Ox

Steed—Monkey

Peach blossom—Rabbit

Dog—Rat

The Rat can't help correcting the Dog's all-too-human errors, which makes the Dog feel belittled and sub par—a disaster from the insecure Dog's point of view. This pairing resembles a parent/child relationship too closely for it to work smoothly.

Dog—Ox

This could be a maudlin pity party waiting to happen, and the double dose of pessimism does neither of these two souls any good. However, the Dog has much compassion for the sweet-natured yet awkward Ox, and this can be a nurturing and loyal relationship.

Dog—Tiger

If ever there were a karmic love affair, it would be between these two souls. The Tiger and the Dog are naturally drawn toward one another and interact with encouragement and generosity. The Tiger is the emperor and the Dog, the prime minister.

Dog—Rabbit

This is a match made in heaven and these two souls recognize each other immediately. This match is so potent that if something were to go wrong between them and they had to part, neither would be likely to recover fully.

Dog—Dragon

Although the Dragon and the Dog are polarized opposites as different as night and day, each possesses traits that the other would do well to learn. Good business associates, but a difficult and complicated love union.

Dog—Snake

Both of these multi-sensorial souls seek to understand the metaphysics of life. They will enjoy many hours together delving into otherworldly knowledge. These two souls are first-rate friends and never run out of interesting topics to discuss.

Dog—Horse

The Dog and the Horse make up a delightful team in friendship and in love. These two souls adore one another and speak the same language of humanity, freedom, and fairness. These two Robin Hoods could very easily find themselves in the middle of a revolution.

Dog—Goat

Both souls tend to be pessimists, and this double dose of cynicism does neither the anxious Dog nor the depressive Goat any good. The Dog herds the Goat into places he has no desire to go, thus bringing out the billy goat's horns.

Dog—Monkey

The Monkey's superb sense of humor and absurdity lifts the Dog out of her frequent bouts of doom and gloom. However, the Monkey can be wickedly naughty sexually, and the Dog rarely forgives such indiscretions.

Dog—Rooster

Each sign antagonizes the other, and a relationship is likely to bring out the worst in both personalities. This is a difficult combination of energies, as the thin-skinned Dog is not equipped to be the recipient of the Rooster's caustic barbs.

Dog—Dog

These two serious souls are very compatible together. Each examines the other through the glasses of proven loyalty. These two natural confidants are well-equipped to support each other through times of anxiety and worry.

Dog—Pig

While they are not found in the traditional triangles of compatibility, these two souls can share a long and happy life together. This pairing makes a loyal and romantic allegiance that can stand the test of time.

鼠牛虎兔龍蛇馬羊猴鶏犬猪

PERFECTLY PERVERTED PIG

Jan 30, 1911 to Feb 17, 1912: Metal Pig
Feb 16, 1923 to Feb 4, 1924: Water Pig
Feb 4, 1935 to Jan 23, 1936: Wood Pig
Jan 22, 1947 to Feb 9, 1948: Fire Pig
Feb 8, 1959 to Jan 27, 1960: Earth Pig
Jan 27, 1971 to Jan 15, 1972: Metal Pig
Feb 13, 1983 to Feb 1, 1984: Water Pig
Jan 31, 1995 to Feb 18, 1996: Wood Pig
Feb 18, 2007 to Feb 6, 2008: Fire Pig
Feb 5, 2019 to Jan 24, 2020: Earth Pig
Needs: affection, physical love
Hates: competition, breaking the rules
Turn-ons: Jacuzzis, hot tubs, bubble baths
Turnoffs: dishonesty

Considerate, gentle, and extremely affectionate, the unpretentious Pig has a simple and pure heart and makes a loyal friend and a sensual lover. This is a soul who needs a generous amount of affection and an earthy, demonstrative lover. Companionship, physical love, and emotional security are a must—Pig men in particular need an easy-going mate who talks out problems instead of shouting. Strong-willed yet sensitive and tenderhearted, they need plentiful physical demonstrations of love.

Holding the last love position in the Zodiac bridging the new cycle, Pigs are gifted at joining fragmented emotions and comforting broken hearts. Monogamous and long-suffering in love, Pigs are honest and supportive lovers who can be counted on for better or for worse. If they are separated from a soul mate or lover, Pigs of both sexes will withdraw deeply into themselves. This is a deeply-feeling partner who is devoted to their mate and able to overlook their inadequacies.

Both male and female Pigs are emotional lovers and seek a close, bonding sexual experience. For this reason, a favorite sexual position is the side-by-side "flying mandarin duck" position, as it is conducive to relaxed, unhurried sex, anal or rear entry play, and other assorted pleasures. The face-to-face "soulmating" position is also a surefire turn-on for male and female Pigs, as it is the best position for direct eye contact and the exchange of yin/yang with each other. The most sensual time for the Pig is during the still and quiet late evening hours between 9 p.m. and 11 p.m.

If your man was born into a Pig year:

The male Pig has an unquenchable desire for physical pleasures. He especially relishes languishing around with his beloved, unhurried and pressure-free. Despite his masculine appearance, the Pig has a feminine, yin soul and knows how to please a woman. His sex appeal is strong to the fairer sex; he seems to understand a woman's mind and body and can even foresee her responses.

While a slow starter in the realm of love and sex, the Pig man quickly makes up for lost time. Love at first sight is possible, but his woman will need some credible credentials as he is a perfectionist at heart. Not every woman will appreciate the fact that his secret "quality assurance measuring stick" is his mother! Any woman he has serious intentions toward will be subconsciously evaluated according to this criterion, and she can be a tough act to follow. The good news is that, because he has such respect and reverence for his mother, he loves women—I mean he *really loves* women. A misogynistic Pig male would be a rare oddity indeed. He treats his woman—and indeed all women—like the queens he believes them to be.

Pig men innately understand the concept of yin/yang exchange between a man and a woman, and are quick to channel their ching qi (raw sexual energy) into an exploration of their lovers. Intuitive and sometimes bordering on the psychic, the Pig male wants to know everything about his lover. It is difficult to keep a secret from this earnest fellow. He has a sexual preference for childlike, dependent females, for it assures him that they will look to him for assistance. The Pig man likes to feel indispensable—when he feels needed, he feels loved.

His bawdy and at times unorthodox sexual tastes can be either a blessing or a curse. A lot depends on how he chooses to channel his erotic energy. The woman earthy enough to engage in a cosmic lovefest with the Pig will find multiple orgasms awaiting her. He is an obliging Babe, our Pig man, and content to wait his turn for fleshly fulfillment. His partner always comes first (pun intended), and her needs and desires become his own.

The Pig man is a faithful lover—which seems to be a contradiction considering his strong libido, but it's true. In addition to his almost unlimited capacity for love and sex, he also has moral principals with a capital P. His loyalty to his lover is unsurpassed, and rarely will he consider breaking off a relationship of any depth. Vulnerable, emotional, and extremely sexual, your Pig man wishes to merge with you completely. Love to him means a complete fusion of spirit, mind, and body, which is why he never suspects that his partner would ever leave their relationship. Of course, in real life breakups do happen, and when this occurs the Pig suffers greatly. If he is romantically wounded or scorned, he is capable of retaliating with childish behavior or even emotional blackmail.

If your woman was born into a year of the Pig:

Sympathetic, sensual, and brimming with sentimentality, the Pig woman is a passive yin lover of the negative, feminine night-force variety. Deeply romantic and intensely emotional, loving and being loved is her lifeblood. She can be a classic princess aching for her prince charming, or a professional woman power-lunching with a tall, dark, and handsome executive. Whatever her leanings or circumstances, the Pig woman wishes to merge with her beloved completely.

Similar to her Pig brother, when the Pig woman feels needed she feels loved. Generally, her problem is not in finding a compatible partner, but in choosing between the many suitors who are drawn to this angel of femininity. Ultra-sensitive and fully vested in her partner, she can be devastated by rejection. Her tender heart does not bounce back quickly from a break. Because of this, she would fare better with an older, more mature partner who is not as prone to change or fickleness. Female Pigs need a dependable and stable man, someone who subconsciously reminds her of her father, whom she idolizes.

Her sex life, while a little compartmentalized ("Tuesday night is sex night"), is always a warm and passionate experience of exceptional quality. She makes a gentle, accommodating, and deeply affectionate lover. Similar to her Pig brothers, her fidelity is beyond reproach and her lover will never have reason to suspect otherwise. Always ready to bring her lover to sexual bliss, she is not sexually demanding; his pleasure is also her pleasure. The demands of children and in-laws at home can make the time and privacy for passionate pleasures a scare commodity. For this reason it is extremely important that married Pigs get away at least once a week for a "date night." So reserve a table for two at her favorite restaurant, or get a hotel room and stock it with candles, bubble bath, and her favorite music. Use your imagination and vary this scenario depending on her tastes.

The Pig female has strong maternal instincts, and she will find deep happiness devoting herself to the welfare of her children and the happiness of her husband. Although she possesses a gentle soul, when it comes to loyalty toward her husband, or if called upon to defend her children, she can and will sprout tusks and become a beastly Babe.

Compatibilities

Romantically, the best match for the Pig is with those born during Goat or Rabbit years; however, their true soul mate is found with the brave Tiger. Be cautious in love relationships with the Snake and Monkey.

Pig (- yin):

Soul mate to—Tiger

In trine with—Horse, Dog

In opposition to—Snake

Combatant to—Monkey

In kind with—Dog

Resolving karma with—Tiger

Steed—Snake

Peach blossom—Rat

Pig—Rat

Rats have a tendency to feel as if nobody understands them, so feeling understood in a love relationship is important for their peace of mind. The compassionate Pig fits the emotional bill.

Pig—Ox

These two calm souls speak the same language of quiet strength and old-fashioned virtues. However, both the Ox and Pig are quiet and solitary souls, so they do not normally gravitate toward each other unless they are introduced by a third party. This could prevent romantic sparks from igniting.

Pig—Tiger

While the Tiger is awesomely compatible with both the Horse and the Dog, it is the honest and affectionate Pig who is the Tiger's soul mate. The resigned Pig truly appreciates the Tiger's sublime qualities, and is never threatened by the Tiger's grand accomplishments. In friendship and in love this relationship is a keeper.

Pig—Rabbit

This is a sweet relationship between two gentle, well-mannered, and genuinely virtuous souls. The diplomatic and socially adept Rabbit aids and befriends the shy Pig to the benefit of both. These two are unmistakably good partners.

Pig—Dragon

Almost everyone gets along well with the sweet-natured Pig, and the Dragon is no exception. A wide and smooth path to romance awaits these two.

Pig—Snake

While both are agreeable and deeply-feeling souls, the Snake and the Pig remain in polarized opposition. The Pig judges the Snake as being less scrupulous than himself, and this drives a wedge between the two. In time, the Snake will tire of the Pig's eternal optimism.

Pig—Horse

The normally peace-loving Pig can become antagonistic and quarrelsome when paired with the Horse. The Pig feels it necessary to constantly correct the Horse, and generally throws a wet blanket on the Horse's parade.

Pig—Goat

A loving relationship of courtesy and respect exists between these two gentle souls. The Goat teaches the Pig about romance and in turn learns temperance from the Pig. Both are good Samaritans and casually take life as it comes.

Pig—Monkey

Given the regularity with which these two souls come together, the natural assumption would be that they are compatible. Unfortunately, this is not the case. Monkeys have their own agenda, which may or may not include the Pig. The Pig stands to get hurt in this union.

Pig—Rooster

Good humor and admiration flourish between the Pig and the Rooster. The Rooster will benefit from the Pig's even temperament, while the Pig encourages the Rooster to express her hidden feelings in safety. This makes for a great relationship.

Pig—Dog

While they are not found in the traditional triangles of compatibility, these two tender souls often celebrate golden wedding anniversaries. This is a loyal and romantic couple able to stand the test of time.

Pig—Pig

Two Pigs together are akin to a committee of ethics and morals. While no couple is perfect, these two come very close. Both are honest and uncomplicated, and desire to fully enjoy the sensual pleasures of life.

CHAPTER 29

鼠牛虎兔龍蛇馬羊猴鷄犬猪

"A Thousand Loving Thrusts": The Chinese Art of Penile Thrusting

WHEN IT COMES TO VAGINAL PENETRATION and sexual intercourse, it is often said, "Stimulate the lotus but do not harm the petals."

The 9 x 10 Thrust Sequence

In this technique, the man alternates between deep and shallow thrusts in the following order:

1. Nine shallow thrusts, using only the tip of the penis head to penetrate.
2. One deep thrust, penetrating the entire vagina.
3. Eight shallow tip penetrations.
4. Two deep, full penetrations.
5. Seven shallow and three deep thrusts.
6. Six shallow and four deep.
7. Five shallow and five deep.
8. Four shallow and six deep.
9. Three shallow and seven deep.
10. Two shallow and eight deep.
11. And finally—one shallow and nine deep thrusts.

It is ideal for the man to accomplish three sets of these 9 × 10 penal thrusting sequences. (Note: This may be so arousing that ejaculation slowing techniques may be called for.)

Soft Entry

There are two techniques for soft entry when the man needs assistance in attaining an erection. The first involves taking his mind and focus off of his penis by bringing his woman to orgasm by way of oral sex. Her cries of ecstasy will serve to distract him nicely (and are a huge turn-on for almost anyone). After this, the woman takes her lover's penis into her mouth and fellates it until it begins to harden. She then continues the sucking while using her tongue to lick the underside of his penis, gradually increasing the strength of the sucking in response to his arousal. This is continued until he has a hard enough erection to make penetration possible.

In the second soft entry technique, the man encircles the base of his penis with his thumb and forefinger. He forms a firm ring with his fingers and "milks" the blood into the shaft and head of the penis, doing so until he is firm enough to penetrate the woman. (This technique is easiest in the male superior position, which uses gravity to fill the penis with blood.) He keeps his fingers around the base of his penis while inserting it, and continues to hold it in this way while thrusting until his erection is fully hardened. In this technique, sufficient lubrication is important for both the man and the woman.

Ten Indications of Female Arousal and Satisfaction

1. When the woman is sexually attracted to a man, her breathing will change and her lips will become dry. She will flush, and the skin on her chest will redden.
2. When a woman looks deeply into a man's eyes, holds the man tightly with both hands, and opens her mouth, she desires him to enter her.
3. A woman wants more clitoral stimulation when she raises her body toward him.
4. A woman is greatly aroused when she begins moving her body and pulling the man toward her using her feet.

5. When she moves from side to side, she desires deeper thrusts from the man.

6. When she crosses her legs behind her partner's back, she is extremely aroused and desires the thrusting to continue.

7. When she desires to reach orgasm, she will hold the man tightly, trembling and sometimes panting, and her voice will be shaky.

8. When her nipples harden and her nose becomes congested, she wants penetration combined with direct clitoral stimulation.

9. When her fluids are very wet and flooding her "jade gate," she desires more intensity, as well as direct clitoral (red lotus) stimulation from his penis until she reaches orgasm ("becoming one with the Tao").

10. A woman is satisfied when her face flushes, her eyes close, and her body tense and relaxes. She will stretch out comfortably, wanting to sleep.

鼠牛虎兔龍蛇馬羊猴鷄犬猪

TAOIST SEXUAL POSITIONS FOR ENGLIGHTENED LOVERS

FOR THE ANCIENT CHINESE, GOOD SEX equaled good health. A satisfying sex life was said to ward off the seven emotional illnesses of depression, fear, anxiety, selfishness, anger, sadness, and remorse.

The *Tao of Loving* is the oldest known sexual manual in existence, predating the *Kama Sutra* (a combination of Taoist sexual techniques and seduction methods described by the Roman poet Ovid) quite significantly. Mongols overran China during the 13th and 14th centuries, and during these years of repression unfortunately destroyed almost all erotic texts. However, the *Tao Te Ching* (the *Book of the Way*, an ancient scripture credited to the sage Laozi) survived, and thankfully it contained these earlier works. The *Secrets of the Jade Bed Chamber*, written during the Han Dynasty (206 B.C. to A.D. 219), is one of the few ancient texts that survived. *The Priceless Recipe*, by Sun S'su-Mo, a 7th-century physician, is another one that has survived antiquity. It contains an ancient "squeeze technique" used to prevent premature ejaculation. This same technique (described in Chapter 29 of this book) was touted as "new" by Masters and Johnson, and is still recommended today by modern sexologists.

There are as many possible ways to make love as there are people. However, most are variations on the six main Chinese sexual positions described in these ancient texts.

Basic Sexual Positions

Man on Top

Considered biologically "natural" in the West, the male superior position was not tops on the sexual hit parade in ancient China. While the face-to-face "missionary" position does allow intimacy, eye contact, and deep thrusting by the man, its drawbacks are difficulty for the man in controlling ejaculation and lack of movement for the woman. This was, however, said to be a good position for conception.

Woman on Top

Commonly depicted in ancient Eastern art, the female superior position allows total control and mobility for the woman and allows her man to relax and enjoy the experience. This position also allows the woman to enact and better understand the male role, as represented by the small dot of white yang within the dark feminine yin half of the tai qi (yin/yang) symbol. Likewise, the man has the opportunity to relate to the female role, as represented by the small speck of dark yin within the white yang half of the tai qi. This was also said to be the best position for a woman to reach orgasm as it allows her to reach and stimulate her clitoris. Each woman's weight, size, and energy level may or may not make this a good choice. A poor position for conception.

Side-by-Side

This is an excellent position for "good morning" casual sex, as well as for tired, pregnant, or convalescing couples. It allows either the man or woman to stimulate the woman's clitoris and provides freedom of movement for both partners. The main drawback is difficult entry into the vagina, especially if the man's penis is of the smaller "valley" or "earthly" jade stem variety. A good position for conception.

Rear Entrance

Sometimes less favored because of its primitive origin and impersonal lack of face-to-face closeness, the rear entry position and its variants can be erotic and fun, and are a favorite of men who love the shape of a woman's buttocks—or who are simply in a dominant mood. This position is good for larger-size couples, men with shorter penises (valley and earthly stems), or women with longer vaginal vaults (jade courtyards). An excellent position for conception.

Sitting

This is a casual and leisurely position, excellent for preliminary lovemaking and foreplay. The woman sits facing the man while straddling his erect penis. A great position for direct eye contact and playful sex, it allows breast play, freedom of movement, and good face-to-face intimacy. The drawbacks are that it doesn't allow enthusiastic thrusting, and the penetration may be too deep for shorter vaginas (jade doors). Not thought to be a good choice for conception.

Standing

This is the position most favored for the mind-blowing "quickie." Each partner stands on one leg while wrapping the other around their partner. This is a wonderful position for spontaneous sex, sex in semi-public places, or as a segueway into sex from sensual dancing. It allows each partner free use of their hands, and is ideal if both lovers are close to the same height. A poor position for conception.

Sexual Positions for Enlightened Lovers

When making love for any sustained period of time, a change of position is important for variety and to prevent muscle cramps. Notice how each position can segue and flow into the next with a quick roll or reversal of places.

Face-to-Face "Soulmating" Position

This is good for when one or both partners are feeling emotional or in need of a close bonding experience. This is also the best position for intense direct eye contact and spiritual oneness with each other.

"Butterfly Clings to Branch"

The man approaches his woman from behind and pulls her arched body closely to him. His left arm encircles her torso, while his right arm helps support the both of them. He then uses the 9 x 10 thrusting sequence from side to side. The woman may also lower herself down and stretch out

flush with the bed, with her arms outstretched directly in front of her. She can then raise her buttocks and tuck her legs beneath her. With both of these variations, the woman inhales and constricts her vaginal muscles tightly as the man enters, then relaxes her muscles and exhales as he withdraws. If the woman's hair is very long, her lover may gently bundle it in his hand, grasping it firmly yet delicately as he would fine silk. This is a good position when the woman is feeling in a submissive mood and wishes her man to take a more assertive role.

"The Lute String"

The woman places a pillow under the man's buttocks and elevates his pelvis to a comfortable height so that he is "served up" nicely for her to go to work. She can kneel between his knees and fellate him, reaching up to play with his nipples very gently at first, and then getting firmer as the man approaches orgasm. Guaranteed to truly blow his mind!

"The Black Pearl"

This is the yin variation of the "lute string." In this position the woman lies on her back with a small pillow under her buttocks. Her lover kneels or lies prone between her legs and takes her clitoris gently in his mouth, sucking and moving up and down her clitoral shaft with the same rhythmic motions he himself would like used on his penis during fellatio. Simultaneously, he inserts his finger about two finger widths deep into her vagina and curls his finger upward to stimulate her G-spot. This combination is absolutely mind-boggling for the woman—not to mention a major turn-on for her lover to give her such pleasure!

"Mandarin Ducks Entwined"

This is a side-by-side position, excellent for relaxed sex, rear entry, anal play, and other assorted pleasures. The woman may tuck her legs up or take her flexed outer leg and place it back over the man. He is then free to hold her leg open, allowing him to penetrate her deeply and giving him easy access to her clitoris.

"The Yin/Yang Communion"

The woman sits facing her lover in his lap and straddles his erect penis, allowing it to penetrate her deeply. This position is ideal for extremely deep penetration and passionate kissing, as well as a feeling of complete oneness. A variation of this is with the couple sitting on the floor or bed while the woman wraps her legs around the man as he supports her back or waist.

"The Peach Blossom"

The woman lies on her back and raises her legs up toward her head. Her man then penetrates her as she brings her legs to rest on his shoulders. He is then free to take either one or both of her legs as they move together with his thrusts. This is one of the positions that allows the woman to stimulate her own clitoris using her favorite touch and bring herself quickly to orgasm. This is a huge turn-on for her lover, who is above her enjoying her pleasure.

"The Little Stream"

(Also called the "diving fish.") The man lies on his back with his legs together and extended out straight. The woman mounts him and sits atop his thighs facing him. As she rests her weight on her knees and legs, she bends her legs and extends them along side of his. She then moves her buttocks forward, gradually allowing the head of his penis to penetrate her. The trick of this technique consists of allowing only shallow penetrations, which the woman controls in whatever way she wants. This teases her man's "jade stem," and results in a powerful orgasm for him.

"The Valley Proper"

(Also called "silkworm spins her cocoon.") The woman wraps her legs around her lover's waist in the male superior position. As she pulls him closely to her she tucks him between her arms and legs as if enveloping him into a deep valley. She can then take the lead and move their fused pelvises in any manner she pleases.

"The Deep Chamber"

The woman lies on her back with her knees positioned up and over her breasts. Her lover kneels over her and penetrates her, gently holding her legs back with both hands. He uses his penis to thrust into her, withdraws and allows it to slide over her clitoris, then inserts it again. He continues this until she reaches orgasm.

"The Inner Door"

The woman lies face down while her man holds her legs. He penetrates her from behind as she raises her buttocks to enjoy the sensations on her labia. She tightens her vaginal muscles as he penetrates her and relaxes as he withdraws.

"The North Pole"

(Also called the "pair of flying ducks" position.) The woman sits backwards straddling her man's erect penis. She is then in a position to gently cup the man's testicles or stimulate him anally. Not only can her lover relax and enjoy himself fully, but he also has an erotic view of her beautiful back, buttocks, and waist curves.

鼠牛虎兔龍蛇馬羊猴鷄犬猪

FIND YOUR CHINESE BIRTH SIGN

Date		Birth Sign	
From	To	Element	Animal
January 30, 1881	February 17, 1882	Metal	Snake
February 18, 1882	January 7, 1883	Water	Horse
February 8, 1883	January 27, 1884	Water	Goat
January 28, 1884	February 14, 1885	Wood	Monkey
February 15, 1885	February 3, 1886	Wood	Rooster
February 4, 1886	January 23, 1887	Fire	Dog
January 24, 1887	February 11, 1888	Fire	Pig
February 12, 1888	January 30, 1889	Earth	Rat
January 31, 1889	January 20, 1890	Earth	Ox
January 21, 1890	February 29, 1892	Metal	Rabbit
January 30, 1892	February 16, 1893	Water	Dragon
February 17, 1893	February 5, 1894	Water	Snake
February 6, 1894	January 25, 1895	Wood	Horse
January 26, 1895	February 12, 1896	Wood	Goat
February 13, 1896	February 1, 1897	Fire	Monkey
February 2, 1897	January 21, 1898	Fire	Rooster

Date		Birth Sign	
From	To	Element	Animal
January 22, 1898	February 9, 1899	Earth	Dog
February 10, 1899	January 30, 1900	Earth	Pig
January 31, 1900	February 18, 1901	Metal	Rat
February 19, 1901	February 7, 1902	Metal	Ox
February 8, 1902	January 28, 1903	Water	Tiger
January 29, 1903	February 15, 1904	Water	Rabbit
February 16, 1904	February 3, 1905	Wood	Dragon
February 4, 1905	January 24, 1906	Wood	Snake
January 25, 1906	February 12, 1907	Fire	Horse
February 13, 1907	February 1, 1908	Fire	Goat
February 2, 1908	January 21, 1909	Earth	Monkey
January 22, 1909	February 9, 1910	Earth	Rooster
February 10, 1910	January 29, 1911	Metal	Dog
January 30, 1911	February 17, 1912	Metal	Pig
February 18, 1912	February 5,1913	Water	Rat
February 6, 1913	January 25, 1914	Water	Ox
January 26, 1914	February 13, 1915	Wood	Tiger
February 14, 1915	February 2, 1916	Wood	Rabbit
February 3, 1916	January 22, 1917	Fire	Dragon
January 23, 1917	February 10, 1918	Fire	Snake
February 11, 1918	January 31,1919	Earth	Horse
February, 1, 1919	February 19, 1920	Earth	Goat
February 20, 1920	February 7, 1921	Metal	Monkey
February 8, 1921	January 27, 1922	Metal	Rooster
January 28, 1922	February 15, 1923	Water	Dog
February 16, 1923	February 4, 1924	Water	Pig
February 5, 1924	January 24, 1925	Wood	Rat
January 25, 1925	February 12, 1926	Wood	Ox
February 13, 1926	February 1, 1927	Fire	Tiger
February 2, 1927	January 22, 1928	Fire	Rabbit
January 23, 1928	February 9, 1929	Earth	Dragon

Date		Birth Sign	
From	To	Element	Animal
February 10, 1929	January 29, 1930	Earth	Snake
January 30, 1930	February 16, 1931	Metal	Horse
February 17, 1931	February 5, 1932	Metal	Goat
February 6, 1932	January 25, 1933	Water	Monkey
January 26, 1933	February 13, 1934	Water	Rooster
February 14, 1934	February 3, 1935	Wood	Dog
February 4, 1935	January 23, 1936	Wood	Pig
January 24, 1936	February 10, 1937	Fire	Rat
February 11, 1937	January 30, 1938	Fire	Ox
January 31, 1938	February 18, 1939	Earth	Tiger
February 19, 1939	February 7, 1940	Earth	Rabbit
February 8, 1940	January 26, 1941	Metal	Dragon
January 27, 1941	February 14, 1942	Metal	Snake
February 15, 1942	February 4, 1943	Water	Horse
February 5, 1943	January 24, 1944	Water	Goat
January 25, 1944	February 12, 1945	Wood	Monkey
February 13, 1945	February 1, 1946	Wood	Rooster
February 2, 1946	January 21, 1947	Fire	Dog
January 22, 1947	February 9, 1948	Fire	Pig
February 10, 1948	January 28, 1949	Earth	Rat
January 29, 1949	February 16, 1950	Earth	Ox
February 17, 1950	February 5, 1951	Metal	Tiger
February 6, 1951	January 26, 1952	Metal	Rabbit
January 27, 1952	February 13, 1953	Water	Dragon
February 14, 1953	February 2, 1954	Water	Snake
February 3, 1954	January 23, 1955	Wood	Horse
January 24, 1955	February 11, 1956	Wood	Goat
February 12, 1956	January 30, 1957	Fire	Monkey
January 31, 1957	February 17, 1958	Fire	Rooster
February 18, 1958	February 7, 1959	Earth	Dog
February 8, 1959	January 27, 1960	Earth	Pig

| Date | | Birth Sign | |
From	To	Element	Animal
January 28, 1960	February 14, 1961	Metal	Rat
February 15, 1961	February 4, 1962	Metal	Ox
February 5, 1962	January 24, 1963	Water	Tiger
January 25, 1963	February 12, 1964	Water	Rabbit
February 13, 1964	February 1, 1965	Wood	Dragon
February 2, 1965	January 20, 1966	Wood	Snake
January 21, 1966	February 8, 1967	Fire	Horse
February 9, 1967	January 29, 1968	Fire	Goat
January 30, 1968	February 16, 1969	Earth	Monkey
February 17, 1969	February 5, 1970	Earth	Rooster
February 6, 1970	January 26, 1971	Metal	Dog
January 27, 1971	February 14, 1972	Metal	Pig
February 15, 1972	February 2, 1973	Water	Rat
February 3, 1973	January 22, 1974	Water	Ox
January 23, 1974	February 10, 1975	Wood	Tiger
February 11, 1975	January 30, 1976	Wood	Rabbit
January 31, 1976	February 17, 1977	Fire	Dragon
February 18, 1977	February 6, 1978	Fire	Snake
February 7, 1978	January 27, 1979	Earth	Horse
January 28, 1979	February 15, 1980	Earth	Goat
February 16, 1980	February 4, 1981	Metal	Monkey
February 5, 1981	January 24, 1982	Metal	Rooster
January 25, 1982	February 12, 1983	Water	Dog
February 13, 1983	February 1, 1984	Water	Pig
February 2, 1984	February 19, 1985	Wood	Rat
February 20, 1985	February 8, 1986	Wood	Ox
February 9, 1986	January 28, 1987	Fire	Tiger
January 29, 1987	February 16, 1988	Fire	Rabbit
February 17, 1988	February 5, 1989	Earth	Dragon
February 6, 1989	January 26, 1990	Earth	Snake
January 27, 1990	February 14, 1991	Metal	Horse

Date		Birth Sign	
From	To	Element	Animal
February 15, 1991	February 3, 1992	Metal	Goat
February 4, 1992	January 22, 1993	Water	Monkey
January 23, 1993	February 9, 1994	Water	Rooster
February 10, 1994	January 30, 1995	Wood	Dog
January 31, 1995	February 18, 1996	Wood	Pig
February 19, 1996	February 6, 1997	Fire	Rat
February 7, 1997	January 27, 1998	Fire	Ox
January 28, 1998	February 15, 1999	Earth	Tiger
February 16, 1999	February 4, 2000	Earth	Rabbit
February 5, 2000	January 23, 2001	Metal	Dragon
January 24, 2001	February 11, 2002	Metal	Snake
February 12, 2002	January 31, 2003	Water	Horse
February 1, 2003	January 21, 2004	Water	Goat
January 22, 2004	February 8, 2005	Wood	Monkey
February 9, 2005	January 28, 2006	Wood	Rooster
January 29, 2006	February 17, 2007	Fire	Dog
February 18, 2007	February 6, 2008	Fire	Pig
February 7, 2008	January 25, 2009	Earth	Rat
January 26, 2009	February 13, 2010	Earth	Ox
February 14, 2010	February 2, 2011	Metal	Tiger
February 3, 2011	January 22, 2012	Metal	Rabbit
January 23, 2012	February 9, 2013	Water	Dragon
February 10, 2013	January 30, 2014	Water	Snake
January 31, 2014	February 18, 2015	Wood	Horse
February 19, 2015	February 7, 2016	Wood	Goat
February 8, 2016	January 27, 2017	Fire	Monkey
January 28, 2017	February 15, 2018	Fire	Rooster
February 16, 2018	February 4, 2019	Earth	Dog
February 5, 2019	January 24, 2020	Earth	Pig

鼠牛虎兔龍蛇馬羊猴雞犬豬

BIBLIOGRAPHY

Chao, Wei-Pang. *Folklore Studies: The Chinese Science of Fate*. Beijing: Calculation Journal, Vol. 5, 1946.

Chatley, Herbert. *The Cycles of Cathay*: *Journal of the Royal Asiatic Society*. The Observatory, Vol. 60, June 1937.

Chia, Mantak. *The Multi-Orgasmic Couple: Sexual Secrets Every Couple Should Know*. San Francisco, Calif.: HarperSanFrancisco, 2000.

Gascoigne, Bamber. *The Treasures and Dynasties of China*. London: Johnathan Cape Ltd., 1973.

Lai, Hsi. *Sexual Teachings of the Jade Dragon: Taoist Methods for Male Sexual Revitalization*. Rochester, Vt.: Destiny Books, 2002.

———. *Sexual Teachings of the White Tigress: Secrets of the Female Taoist Masters*. Rochester, Vt.: Destiny Books, 2001.

Sung, Edgar. *Ten Thousand Years Book*. San Francisco, Calif.: MJE Publishing, 2003.

Vaknin, Sam. *Malignant Self-Love: Narcissism Revisited*. Prague: Narcissus Publications, 2006.

Wang, Lihua. *Chinese Home Remedies: Harnessing Ancient Wisdom for Self-Healing*. Franklin Lakes, N.J.: New Page Books, 2005.

Wu, Shelly. *Chinese Astrology: Exploring the Eastern Zodiac*. Franklin Lakes, N.J.: New Page Books, 2005.

Zettnersan, Chian. *Taoist Bedroom Secrets: Tao Chi Kung*. Translated by Christine M. Grimm. Twin Lakes, Wis.: Lotus Press, 2002.

鼠牛虎兔龍蛇馬羊猴雞犬猪

INDEX

A

adult toys, 133
American Psychiatric Association, 84
anal sex, 134
antisocial personality disorder, 86
aphrodisiacs, herbal, 108
aromatherapy, 99-101
Art of the Jade Bedchamber, 116
Asian Zodiac, 13
atmosphere, 99-111
avoidant personality disorder, 86-87

B

bath oil recipes, 101-102
birth sign, finding your, 237-241
birth, 121-123
black pearl position, 231
borderline personality disorder, 87-88
butterfly clings to branch position, 230

C

candles, seduction and, 102
carrier oil, 100
character, importance of, 12-13
China, Ancient, 12
China, masturbation in, 132
Chinese Zodiac, 12 signs of, 109
ching qi, overview of, 115
Ching, Su Nu, 125
colors, seduction and, 102
compatibility, 50-52
conception, 121-123
concubine, definition of, 117
Confucius, 83
consort, definition of, 117
control, ejaculation, 125, 126
courtesan, definition of, 117
deep chamber position, 234
deep kissing, 116

鼠牛虎兔龍蛇馬羊猴鷄犬猪

ABOUT THE AUTHOR

LIKE MOST OF THOSE BORN INTO a year of the defending Dog, Shelly Wu spent a fair amount of her childhood fighting bullies and taking up the gauntlet for the picked on and the friendless. Shelly no longer scuffles with bullies, but she still maintains her soapboxes. She adheres to the teaching of Laozi: "In the perception of the smallest is the secret of clear vision; in the guarding of the weakest is the secret of all strength."

Those who have met Shelly Wu say she has a certain "spark" that is unmistakable. Using an eclectic mixture of metaphysics and psychology, she has been dubbed the "Dear Abby" of Chinese astrology. Wu's horoscope columns and feature articles have appeared in *aMagazine: Inside Asian America*, *The Rainbow News*, *Psychic Interactive*, *Your Stars*, *InTouch*, and *LIFE* magazine. Her articles have been featured by the Associated Press, ABC News, the BBC, and Wireless Flash news services.

In 1995, she brought this ancient art to the World Wide Web, and continues to maintain the popular website, *www.chineseastrology.com*. She is also the author of *Chinese Astrology: Exploring the Eastern Zodiac* (New Page Books, 2005), and can be heard on radio talk shows worldwide.